GET OUT OF DEBT FAST, AVOID SCAMS AND INCREASE YOUR CREDIT SCORE!

PAY OFF YOUR CREDIT CARDS IN AS LITTLE AS 18 MONTHS WHILE LEARNING TO IMPROVE YOUR MONEY MANAGEMENT SKILLS

G. S. BOTTOMS

CONTENTS

INTRODUCTION

I've always been good with money. At least I thought I was. It wasn't until one night heading out to dinner with friends while checking my bank account it hit me and struck me hard. I was broke, dead broke. Not only did I have a zero balance, but I had dug such a deep hole of debt I remember thinking I would never get out. I was embarrassed that I had to cancel my dinner plans and even more ashamed that I didn't know what to do next, but I had to start doing something. How did I get here? Were my spending habits that bad? I started asking a lot of questions and doing a lot of searching. There was minimal information I could find to offer up options. Every plan I found had some excellent ideas, but there was always something I would have to sacrifice that didn't make sense long term. I had to pay this back and fast while still focusing on my credit score.

Being in deep debt is no fun. You want to travel, have all these experiences and live carefree. You get tired of stressing about your bills and which you pay first. Choosing between needs for yourself and your family is a hard place due to your debt. It can take a toll on you emotionally and everyone in your life when money is tight. Your decisions become even more brutal, and your relationships become harder to keep happy. Is money the key to our happiness? It isn't but understanding how to manage your income is!

Well, imagine never thinking about your bills or when they are due—just focusing on one thing at a time and seeing results. Even better, imagine every three months having a moment to celebrate carefree from whatever your financial situation currently is. Taking the stress out of your life impacts your emotional state and improves your relationships.

The money topic stops leading to arguments using these strategies, and after reading this book, it won't even be a topic you consider hard to discuss anymore. If anything, your new world might evolve where and how you spend it. A vacation versus a home renovation is the type of debate I can get behind!

This book will teach you how to relieve your bills' stress and show you how to focus on getting out of debt. Once you are out of debt will also learn how to stay out forever! You will learn sound money management and never be late paying a bill again. I was debt-free ($54,731) in less than 18 months without sacrificing my sanity!

I have had the unfortunate experience of not understanding how to leverage what was available until the third time I got into debt. That was by far the deepest hole I had gotten into with my debt. That last journey of being debt-free was by far the most successful of getting out and staying out. The combination of methods I used I share with you and the checklists keeps me out of debt. Being debt-free changes your life, and maintaining it makes it even more rewarding. Your mindset when making decisions moves to a higher level when your debt isn't weighing you down. It was a journey I would repeatedly do as I have gained so much knowledge, and my connections with those I love most have grown incredibly strong. What I cover, no one teaches, and you will learn why as you read through each chapter. I accomplished being debt-free, buying a home, getting a promotion, actually have some savings, and buying a better car all in under 18 months. I never filed for bankruptcy, and I encourage you to read through this thoroughly if that is an option you have considered. You will find that it hurts you more than it helps you long-term. One of the biggest takeaways on this journey was learning there is good debt and bad debt. If you have no one paying your debt, then all of your debt is bad debt like mine. Be ready to answer some tough questions as we start this journey together!

HOW DID I GET HERE?

"We hide our demons so good, that the angels we show, bare the shame on their faces."

— ANTHONY LICCIONE

There is a reason you have amassed debt. The first step in this process is being honest with yourself and understanding you, and you alone created this reality you live in by making this debt. If you are blaming anyone but yourself, this process will take so much longer than it needs to. Admitting to yourself and understanding why you made those decisions will be the winning strategy to never making those decisions again without being fully prepared for an outcome you do not desire.

It may be due to love, duty, or a whole variety of reasons that brought you to this debt hole. Maybe that emergency wasn't an emergency, and had you thought out a different solution, it may have been just a temporary inconvenience. This first step is the hardest part of getting and staying out of debt. I don't think we choose to lie to ourselves or others, only that it is the easy way out. If all the good things in the world were easy, everyone would be doing it. It is easy to blame others instead of owning your reality, but the downside to this method of blaming others creates a deeper hole for you to run circles in pointing fingers. You may have a hole so deep you do not think there is a way for you to get out, but there is. Clever work and persistence will get you out. Yes, some of the work will be hard, but once you finish this book and achieve your goals, the hard part of this will be a memory. Most decisions you make throughout this journey will be temporary but worth the sacrifice. Some of those sacrifices will teach you lessons leading to permanent changes that you choose not because it's what you have to do but what you want to do. This information will be the methodology you can live by for getting and staying out of debt.

We live in a microwave society where our patience is at an all-time low. Due to our lack of patience, we pay for our imPAYtience. I hope the last word's spelling in the prior sentence speaks to you. When you wait out your options and go with what works best for your budget, your PAYtience pays off. Being honest with yourself takes time and involves you asking yourself questions about how you got here and how you get out.

Ask yourself how many feet do you have? We all know the answer, yet millions of people have enough pairs of shoes, boots, or sneakers to pay their monthly bills for a minimum of three months. When you are not in debt, have all the footwear your heart desires. However, if you are in a hole, how many pairs helped you get there.

In a microwave society, the most dangerous tool is your credit card. We want everything now and can't wait long enough to seek a better option or have the actual money to make the purchase. Your impulse purchases end up going unused and start collecting dust. Ever go through your closet and notice an item with the tag still on it? You probably bought it at a great sale, but if you didn't plan on making good use of it anytime soon, you could have held out for a better version of what you bought and not swipe your credit card. There is a lot to gain by understanding how you will benefit from your purchases. Buying items on impulse may feel good at the moment, but then it can quickly put you in a spot where you can no longer afford to make those impulse purchases now that you have gotten into so much debt. There is nothing wrong with getting what you want, but it is essential to remember the actual value it will bring you long term. Like I said in the beginning, honesty with yourself is vital. If you want to shy away from friends and family regarding your financials, so be it but DO NOT shy away from you! Once you can be honest, sharing your story with loved ones can be helpful and supportive during the process.

Honesty starts with admitting where you are. There may also be some terms you are not familiar with that can help you understand where you are and how you begin your journey. You may not be reading this because you are looking to become a real estate tycoon or looking to become the year's subsequent small business, although this information would still help. Ask yourself what the goal you hope to achieve is? Maybe you want to be tighter on your finances or have bigger aspirations to own your own business or home. Whatever it is, this book is the first step to achieving it.

Have you ever heard of the phrase "disposable income"? According to the dictionary, "disposable income is the income remaining after deduction of taxes and other mandatory charges, available to be spent or saved as one wishes." In other words, after you have paid everyone, you owe this is what you have left to make decisions with, to spend freely. The additional mandatory charges are your monthly expenses. I find that monthly expenses are where folks get stuck on maximizing their income. Again, back to honesty, what do you consider to be monthly expenses? How do you decide what you need versus what you want when thinking about your expenses? Don't stress about all the questions I ask. As you answer them, you will understand how this strategy changes your life and finances. How you spend your money is essential, and most of us had to, unfortunately, learn the hard way. On the last page of each chapter, I will list the questions asked and always have the last page as a reference point on your journey. I encourage you to reread them throughout, as this is not an overnight exercise. It takes time to pay off debt, and the time it takes is primarily up to you and how you plan to implement the information I provide. Now that we talked about honesty, we can start to dive into your reality. Have you been able to admit to yourself how you feel about your current reality? Everyone reading this will have a different answer depending on how deep your debt hole is or how quickly you seek to get out. It's not just admitting to yourself you are in a bind but also what are you willing to do to get out of debt? We will cover multiple strategies in this book and the outcome they produce. I offer various methods to correlate with what you are willing to do directly. The different options explained are why understanding your reality and admitting to yourself is so crucial as it will guide you to leverage what will work best for your current reality. If some of you answered that you feel upset, that's good. Turn that energy into ambition and make debt your enemy to conquer. On the opposite, those of you out there feel happy you admitted where you are and look forward to the start of your journey, then awesome. Utilize that positive energy to challenge yourself to reach your goals even faster. The questions you ask yourself will remain the cornerstone while you are on this journey. As you become more honest with yourself and as your reality changes, the answers will change. Never lose sight of your goal. There will be a great deal of knowledge you will learn along the way, and an open mind can be your best friend.

How quickly do you want your reality to change? I often find that the answer to this question determines how far you are willing to use the strategies I offer. The instant solution is as far as you need to; however, when the math starts to explain the hole's depth, people can quickly get discouraged. Begin the process now in this chapter and the next, preparing for what you are willing to do. Don't worry! None of my strategies involve anything illegal or difficult to accomplish. They are all built around your mental and emotional space to make decisions based on your outcome's speed. Time is valuable, and it is yours to use as you best see fit.

These attributes can be improved and magnified as you start your journey with humility. You might ask how humility plays into paying off your debt. The answer is simple it can speed up the time in which you complete your journey and improve your mental and emotional space. By definition, humility is "a modest or low view of one's importance" in the dictionary. I have often discussed this word amongst friends and colleagues to understand better what humility means to them. Some attribute it as the opposite of arrogance, while others recognize it's how you can interact with other people. Attempting not to go too deep into humility and what it may mean for you, the purpose of humility regarding debt is how well you utilize the resources around you. Those resources can be a spouse, family, friends, and neighbors. While none of these people in your life may know how deep your debt hole is doesn't mean they can also not be a part of the journey. Practicing humility can be the defining timeline of paying the debt off six months or potentially by yourself in 2 years. I am grateful for my sister and the support she has provided me on all three of my journeys. By the third time, she was asking me more questions, but with the lessons I had learned, I had a plan and was able to show her my timeline of being debt-free and how I was going to stay out. I accomplished so much with her support and friendship. I never asked her for money, and I completed my goals. There is someone in your life like my sister, and if you have more than one of those people, you will accomplish your goals quickly! As we continue through this book, I will share when she came into supporting me and how I could benefit and increase my timeline in achieving my goals. My last journey out of the debt hole was an experience I would never trade-in. I paid off all my debt, bought a house, got promoted at work, and managed to increase my savings for "emergencies" all in under a year. I was over $54,731 in debt. My last two debt journeys were both separately over $30,000. I hope this inspires you to know this can be done and change your life forever.

Now that you have finished the chapter, I encourage you to keep a journal or take notes of your answers to the questions asked listed below. We will review these questions again throughout the book.

- How many feet do you have?
- What is the goal you hope to achieve?
- Ever heard of the phrase "disposable income"?

- What do you consider to be monthly expenses?
- How do you decide what you need versus what you want when thinking about your expenses?
- Have you been able to admit to yourself how you feel about your current reality?
- What are you willing to do to get out of debt?
- How quickly do you want your reality to change?

2

HOW TO CREATE A FINANCE TEAM FOR FREE!

"You must gain control over your money or the lack of it will forever control you."

— DAVE RAMSEY

Your Finance Team starts with you creating a second bank account. I know what you are thinking. If I am struggling to manage one bank account, how does a second help? The second helps in supporting the mental and emotional space. Remember, the act of paying bills and managing money is a hot topic for everyone. Money is the number one reason relationships and marriages don't work out in the long run, so imagine creating a structure that removes that challenge from your life permanently? I said in the beginning, the methodology in this book will get out of debt and keep you out of debt, and two bank accounts are the foundation of this strategy. You don't have to be picky about where you open the second account, however a few recommendations. If you have more than two personal bank accounts, you should close anything additional and remain with two. Splitting your money up for multiple reasons keeps you from maximizing your dollars. I will always recommend a credit union over a bank any day of the week. A few reasons: they have fewer fees when using their services, the minimum needed to open an account is incredibly smaller, and they typically do not require you to have a high minimum in the account monthly, and did I mention they have better interest rates on loans??? A credit union might only need less than $20 to open an account and $20 to be kept in to maintain your account monthly. A bank will have a minimum of $100 to open and be held in the account. That might not be a big difference to you, but that is money that can be contributing to you paying off your debt. Also, the loan piece may come into play depending on what your current debt hole looks like, and it could be the only downside credit unions have as they do not offer high dollar amounts for personal loans. If you are married, I recommend getting a joint account with your spouse as the second account. Depending on how you currently manage your monthly expenses with your spouse, this may be new for both of you; however, it can help you both whether you split all bills together or someone owns specific bills while the other pays the rest of the bills.

This second bank account is the first step that you must complete before continuing in this book. We have covered how we got here, and now it is time for action. Before you move on to the next chapter, complete this step. Put the book down, go to your local credit union and open an account, whether it be personal or joint with your spouse, and then come back right where you left off as I am waiting for you! Seriously I am trying to be supportive so get 'em, tiger!!!

Ok, now that you have opened the second account, we will discuss the concept. Each chapter will always reference the mental and emotional space of our decisions. What is the difference between you and a Fortune 50 company? They have a finance team. A finance team balances the books, makes decisions on spending, and pays for what is needed and wanted from a company based on revenue. You don't have a finance team now, but that doesn't mean you can't structure your finances similar to a Fortune 50 company. The first step to building this structure is building your finance team through your second bank account. It will help you decide on what is needed, what is wanted, and balance your books. How does this work? Your finance team or bill account will take your revenue (which is your income) and pay for what is needed. Now you might not be able to transfer everything at once based on where you are financially, but over time, within a few months, you should be able to have all of your monthly expenses paid through your bill account through auto-pay.

We will cover income and expenses in the next chapter in more depth but managing your finances like a Fortune 50 company is the key to your financial success and money management. Not all Fortune 50 companies manage their finances 100% this way. However, this concept will help you long-term with making your financial decisions, getting out of debt, and staying out of debt. Think of it as an automated finance team. Fortune 50 companies aren't typically paying all bills monthly either. Some charges are bi-yearly and yearly, saving money on the overall payment due. Think of your car insurance or life insurance. Both show you what the term cost is versus the monthly cost. You can save a monthly payment or more by paying it upfront for the year. Leveraging this structure plans for that and helps you save money in payments over time.

I mentioned I accomplished a lot on that last run to being debt-free. Part of that was my savings. This method helped me achieve that. It also helped me realize I didn't need the amount savings as I thought. Specific bills fluctuate like your utilities throughout the year. Depending on where you live, your heat bill may go through the roof during the winter but drop down in the summer. Same for your electricity when using air conditioning in the summertime. Understanding these fluctuations help to ensure you not only have every dollar needed when you support your bill account, but it is how you can create your savings along the way without sacrificing your disposable income. There are Fortune 50 companies that pay quarterly bonuses to all of their employees based on performance. This strategy is the same exercise you will do every three months. It will help you build savings and help you move through your debt timeline faster. Once you are out of debt, this will help with other goals. Maybe you want to take a lavish trip or renovate a part of your home. This structure in managing your money allows your finance team to assist with that decision and create a timeline. A Fortune 50 company reinvests their excess dollars into themselves through research and development. They also reinvest in their employees – certainly not saying your family is an employee to you, but you get the idea! That's your family vacation! It's similar to that and can be used based on the goals you have set for yourself.

Not 100% of your bills will offer autopay. Thanks to the age of technology, most companies do, but for instance, your landlord might not. Not to worry, credit unions provide a "Bill Pay" program to automatically send a check to who you designate and when you tell them automatically and every month. Imagine being in a space where you don't have to worry about paying your bills because your credit union and the companies you use have agreed to manage it for you. You might not see it now, but this exercise alone, once fully completed, will begin to change how you manage your money. Life is very different when due dates and amounts are of no concern to you. Your life becomes incredibly stable to your income, and most importantly, if anything changes, you know what is needed to maintain your bills every month. If you are embarking on this journey and hope to one day create passive income to cover your expenses, this step helps you understand your goal setting. For those wanting to make career moves, whether it be by choice or for another reason, you have now isolated your needs in one place. Now I don't recommend throwing everything on auto-pay just yet. We will cover that in-depth in the next chapter.

Step 1: Open your second account

After reading this chapter have any of your answers in the first chapter changed? Ask yourself why have they changed.

- What is the goal you hope to achieve?
- Ever heard of the phrase "disposable income"?
- What do you consider to be monthly expenses?
- How do you decide what you need versus what you want when thinking about your expenses?
- Have you been able to admit to yourself how you feel about your current reality?
- What are you willing to do to get out of debt?
- How quickly do you want your reality to change?

3

UNDERSTANDING YOUR EXPENSES VS INCOME

"Don't tell me where your priorities are. Show me where you spend your money and I'll tell you what they are."

— JAMES W. FRICK

Now we are getting to the good stuff. Your debt reflects the decisions you have made regarding your income and expenses. If your costs exceed your income, you go into debt. If your wants exceed your disposable income, you use the credit card, and now you are in debt. When you want something new and take out a loan, you go into debt. So many ways to get into debt, but every decision leads back to your spending habits. Most people think by increasing their income it will fill the debt hole, but sadly, this generally does not happen. When a person's income increases, they typically increase their expenses since now, they can afford more on paper. Do not get trapped by this notion.

Let's talk about income. When you fill out a loan or a credit card, the question is how much you make. The question that you should ask is how much you take home. I will use round numbers to illustrate this example. By all means, follow along with a calculator if needed and look at the impact. If you receive $60,000 a year, your federal tax bracket is a little over 20%, but we will use exactly 20% for this example. If you receive $60,000, you only take home $48,000. That is a $12,000 difference from what you just put on paper to apply for a loan and what you take home to use. This example means whatever maximum you just qualified for can quickly put you in the hole by 20% of your income. Keep in mind that's only looking at the federal tax rate. If you include state tax, city/local tax, Medicare, and social security, that $48,000 becomes much less depending on where you live. You must understand the actual bottom line for your income to make better decisions in your spending habits and stay out of debt. This concept is your gross income versus your net income. While your company pays you $60,000, you do not receive that amount to spend. I don't recommend giving a different number than what you make but understand how to weigh the options when you are approved by whoever for an amount, let's say a $20,000 loan and the impact on your disposable income. It's all fun and games until credit cards are maxed out, and you have minimum payments up to your eyeballs. Your income is essential to you as it is how you maintain your current lifestyle and accomplish your goals. It is also imperative to understand your income and its true purchase power. Always remember you can have what you want. It's the decisions you make with your money that help you achieve that goal without drowning in debt.

Do you need to increase your income to achieve your goals? No, but it makes the journey a shorter one and, it's a decision up to you. You will know more about yourself and what your journey will hold as you continue through this book. Keep in mind that there is a whirlwind of ways to increase your income. My recommendations for increasing your income are temporary since this book's goal is to pay off debt; however, based on what you experience and learn on your journey, it is always your choice to make the change. As we focus on the income, most pay frequency is twice a month, while some receive weekly pay. The money you receive on the check for working 40 or 80 hours is the number you will be using in this next exercise. These checks represent the dollar amount after taxes, medical benefits, or whatever company program you are enrolled in that automatically takes their money, basically your net income. Again, working with whole numbers, if your pay frequency is bi-weekly, multiply that number by two and if you receive pay weekly, multiply that number by 4. Let's say our take-home weekly is $500 or bi-weekly $1000. This calculation means each month our amount is $2000. This step shows our income, and if we multiply our monthly revenue by 3, that equals $6000, which is what we are working with quarterly. Multiply our monthly income by 12, and we can rely on $24,000 yearly.

Yes, there are "extra" pay weeks, 2 for bi-weekly people and 4 for our weekly people, but we do not want to rely on these checks at the moment. If you can focus your financial attention on this whole number method, we are almost there. A tip for you if your check is $500.78 or $1000.97, don't round up, round down, and maintain whole numbers as we continue through this exercise to build out how we are planning to use our income. How much do you take home monthly? Quarterly? Yearly? I will add a breakout of how everything should look at the end of this chapter.

Expenses, expenses, expenses. You might disagree with what I consider expenses but hear me out and keep an open mind. According to the dictionary, an expense is "the cost required for something; the money spent on something". Basically, how much you have to pay for a need or a want. I define expenses as needs only and are reoccurring monthly, meaning unless I no longer need them, the expense will more than likely be there for however long I am on this earth. I also would like to note that I consider my mortgage a need because it is my shelter, even though my mortgage is a debt. You will notice a mortgage is something I leave out of most of this content; however, please note all strategies taught in this book can help you pay your mortgage off in a shorter amount of time. Needs are typically considered food, clothing, and shelter; however, this is where we go down the slippery slope of our spending habits. Let's start with food. Food is 100% a need, but how much of it and what kind? I slip in and out of vegan or backyard barbecue as a diet every week. I keep my ordering out to a minimum, understand your money can float away very quickly, especially in this new age where they deliver everything! Honestly, I blew money on going out to eat before at restaurants when the new delivery apps weren't even a thought, and it was by far one of the biggest challenges I had to overcome due to my love for food. The introduction of apps such as DoorDash and UberEats was a nice confirmation that I had grown. I gave in to temptation a few times, but now I budget for it into my lifestyle while still keeping my usage low.

Ask yourself how much do you spend on take-out? This expense is an item I do not include in my monthly payments or managed by the "finance team". Since this is 100% my decision, I separate it and lock in a budget based on my goals. If paid bi-weekly, I would only budget $250. I would never exceed my budget and bought my groceries weekly. The number is 100% up to you. However, a few questions to check yourself on the number: Do you enjoy your cooking? Do you find yourself throwing out food, whether it expired or was old leftovers? What is it about pre-made meals or take out you enjoy most? These questions should help you understand where at least some of your disposable income is already going. Create a weekly menu. You will be surprised how much you can do with maintaining your tastebuds and appetite! Planning your menu with your family can be a new fun activity if you haven't already started. Who doesn't love Taco Tuesday? Creating a menu with your family helps maintain costs and offers an opportunity to prepare in advance if the recipe allows for it. You and your family will love several popular $10 meals. You can give your kids something to look forward to, and they can still have their favorites at a lower cost. Whether you choose to make it from scratch or purchase pre-made meals will make for the most cost-effective option.

Clothing is a big one, who doesn't want to be fashionable, right? Having the newest clothes and making sure your colors are in and not out for the season is very expensive. I had personally gone through 4 wardrobes as I learned more about myself and how I wanted to have an image when I walked into a room. Most people consider me incredibly fashionable, and I am often asked for tips by both men and women. My passion for fashion is why I know this will be a tough one for many of you to work through. Your style and how you view yourself are essential. I challenge you to think about what you see in the mirror and why it is important. A few recommendations I will make and one question to get you started here. Ladies and gentlemen, I recommend getting what you find most polished and fitting to wear to a wedding only. Only make this purchase if you have nothing already in your closet and just when you need it until you complete paying off your debt. Make sure it is something that you can easily accessorize with so that if you have multiple events, you can be comfortable wearing it a second or third time. I have a faithful navy-blue suit that is my go-to and have numerous accessories, some as low as a $1 purchase that served me well during my interview process for my promotion. No matter what anyone says, you can never be over-dressed. When an occasion such as a gala or a wedding comes up, we are quick to break the bank on being the best dressed there, but with a bit of soul searching, you will find you can be the best dressed at the lowest cost. My question for you: Why is someone else's name more important than your goals? Before you answer, consider this, a name does not always mean there is quality in the product, only popularity. A name does not always improve its functionality, just its popularity. Whoever are you trying to be popular for, I ask you, who is paying your debt? Although this one will be tough again, there is a lot of wiggle room here! I do not include this in my monthly expenses. I have taken the time to build my wardrobe during the best sales and have enjoyed the clearance sections and their rewards. Do not under-estimate the value you can find. Keep in mind just because it is on sale doesn't mean you buy it when it's not needed. Have a plan to enjoy your purchases.

Last but certainly not least, shelter! This need is one of my favorites, as this is where you can gain a lot of traction. Both for the homeowner or renter, the family of four, or the self-serving individual, it is here where our decisions have a lot of long-term impacts on our disposable income. Some items to be considered, if you purchased a home with the highest amount you qualified for in a loan, chances are you are house poor. The scenario is by far one of the easiest to get into debt because you have reduced your disposable income by so much the bulk of your money constantly recycles back to your home. You get the kids toys for the backyard, the house, bath time, and on top of your kids, the parents need toys too! Whether it be decorations for the hallway or a new toolset to use in the garage, it is here where we see imPAYtience hit hard. The significant upside to the homeowners, whether they are house poor or not, is they are building equity and, at some point, will have solidified their shelter in paying off their mortgage. Before we move on from the mortgage topic, I do not recommend chasing paying off your mortgage first as it is typically the giant pill to chew out of your debt. Once all other debt you owed has been paid off, I hope you accept the challenge of shaving years off of your mortgage payments as it is then that the chase can begin. Houses have more upkeep and maintenance than renters have, but you also have different options than a renter may have, depending on the space you rent with your house's current layout. How can you make your house contribute with you? You can earn income from your home to contribute to paying off your debt. You probably didn't purchase your place to share it with a stranger. However, it's a decision entirely up to you to make. The upside is you don't have to do anything forever, and that short-term sacrifice can mean the difference between months and years.

Renting is great for experiencing an area you may want to purchase a home in the future. Maybe it's close to your job, cutting down your commute, or another reason that pulled you into living in the area. Renting, if you compare the square footage in the same neighborhood, is typically higher of an expense than that of a mortgage. My mortgage now is half of what I was paying in rent, and I only live 15 minutes away from the area I was renting. When I was renting in this neighborhood three blocks away from my home, I wanted to buy a house very badly because I knew my mortgage, including home owner's insurance and property taxes, would be half of what I was paying in rent. At the time, I was in my second journey of debt, which was deep. Buying a house now may not be in your cards at this very minute due to your debt, credit score, or savings for a down payment. However, it's a long-term thought to consider. If you are still renting and don't have plans to settle down soon, then become the landlord and the tenant and invest in a duplex or triplex! Just a thought. Similar to the home-owner, you, too, if your lease allows, can rent space as well. Maybe it's a one-bedroom so you might have to make a more considerable sacrifice, but again it's all your decision. The more significant advantage is that once your lease is up, you can move to an apartment with lower rent or, depending on the amount left of your debt, work towards purchasing the duplex, triplex, or home.

You also have the opportunity to practice humility again here by moving in with a relative. Depending on your family structure, you want to ensure it is a loved one supporting your journey. This one can have a massive impact on you mentally and emotionally as you will naturally build a stronger bond with that relative. Even though I had gotten out of debt, I decided to move in with my sister's family during my house hunting process to increase my savings for the down payment and closing costs. It was one of the best experiences I could ask for as the benefit has been ever-lasting. We had our moments as anyone would staying with a loved one, but the outcome was a stronger bond with my sister, brother-in-law, and nephew, who now always wants to hang out with me! This experience was not the first time I had lived with a relative to accomplish a big savings goal. When working towards purchasing my first house, I spent six months living with my grandfather, which changed my life forever. He is now like a best friend, and I bought my current home around the corner from him to easily enjoy his company. Both times I made sure to contribute to the household with a small monthly contribution and chipped in with chores around the home. It will increase your ability to pay off your debt. I do not make the property investment advice or live with relatives for homeowners. You will be required to have a higher down payment for a second property where a non-homeowner will be able to take advantage of this purchase and also, why move in with relatives when you have your own home? You can still benefit from your home for my home-owners in how you choose to share it. With that said, both rent and mortgages are needs. Everyone needs to have shelter, and it is typically an amount charged to you that does not change often. Yes, escrow can impact your mortgage payment, and yes, your landlord can decide to raise your rent, but you will still have options to manage those changes based on the strategies I offer in this book.

Now that we have covered that piece, you will understand why we label needs versus wants the way that we will in this next step. I will ask that you have a notebook, piece of paper, or familiar with excel or google sheets that will work as well. First, we will begin to list the highest monthly bill from the first line down, starting with the monthly payment. Title what the bill is in one column, and here we will round up the monthly payment due. For example, if the bill is $197.22, list the bill as $198. Now multiply each monthly bill listed by the number 3 and create a column next to your title. After you have completed that step add another column and multiply each monthly bill listed by the number 12, and remember always to keep whole numbers rounding up. Now we have a view of where our money has to go monthly, quarterly and yearly. The yearly number might be alarming depending on where you are paying off your debt. Add your totals at the bottom for your monthly, quarterly, and annual. Next, write in your monthly net income next to the word monthly and repeat that step for your quarterly and yearly net income. It is here that we begin our strategy.

Monthly $4000	Bill	Quarterly $12,000	Yearly $48,000
$950	Rent	$2,850	$11,400
$350	Car	$1,050	$4,200
$320	Credit Card	$960	$3,840
$300	Personal Loan	$900	$3,600
$275	Credit Card	$825	$3,300
$175	Car Insurance	$525	$2,100
$120	Cell Phone	$360	$1,440
$100	Cable	$300	$1,200
$100	Personal Loan	$300	$1,200
$60	Electric	$180	$720
$55	Gas	$165	$660
$30	Water	$90	$360
$2,835		**$8,505**	**$34,020**

Now, remember in the beginning that $60,000 a year gross pay is $48,000 after just Uncle Sam comes to grab his share. This $48,000 divided by 12 is $4000 a month. In this example, we pay more than half of our net income in just bills. That is over 50% of what we take home gone only to bills. We haven't even eaten yet! This real-life situation is how we can quickly get into debt. You may be thinking to yourself that you can cancel 1 or 2 items on the list, but the rest are absolute needs! Yes, there are funda-mental needs listed here, but your choices can reduce the price without losing quality or service.

Spending over 50% of your monthly income on just what you owe is a challenging hole to be in, and I am sure some of you reading this are probably paying more than 50% of your income to your monthly expenses. This reality is how we get caught up using credit cards and taking out loans for our wants. You can do the math for yourself to see what your current percentage is.

Take your monthly bills and divide them by your monthly income. Example: 2835/4000=0.708, roughly 71% of your revenue going to monthly bills. What percentage should my monthly expenses be? Although I cannot answer that for you, I can certainly help you understand how to define it for yourself, and it's pretty simple. How much disposable income do you want to enjoy? I like a high amount of disposable income as it fits my lifestyle. Therefore, my monthly expenses are only 25% of my monthly/yearly net pay. The maximum I will go is 30%. I have made my financial decisions based on my experience with debt. The higher my monthly percentage, the lower my disposable income was.

When I wanted to do more, I did not have the additional money to do it and would use a credit card or take a loan to keep up with my wants. When I focused on how I managed my needs financially, it became easier to get out of debt and stay out of debt. For the most part, you currently tend to your wants and how you want to maintain a particular lifestyle. If your spending exceeds your income, you will always come back to dig another debt hole. Remember, I stated two things at the beginning of this chapter and book. I increased my savings and realized I didn't need to save as much as I thought. I only realized this when I was able to recognize my disposable income. Instead of keeping thousands and thousands in the bank, I save what I need in the event of an emergency. I can work through almost any hardship I am challenged with between my disposable income and savings. By recognizing this, I don't have to over-extend my finances to increase my savings. Once I hit that number, I no longer have to account for my savings goal. This step may not be something you are comfortable with as I know plenty of big savers but keep in mind your money could be doing something for you. Fortune 50 companies are not saving boatloads; they are holding; however, they also invest it in themselves. At the beginning of this chapter, I mentioned that people think increasing their income will solve the debt hole; however, sadly, this does not always happen.

Managing to a percentage helps keep your spending in check even if your income increases. A pay increase can bring a feeling of euphoria where you buy a new car, take a lavish vacation all on credit before you get to see what the net pay for that promotion is. You may have received a $10,000 raise but keep in mind depending on how you get paid, whether it be weekly or bi-weekly, Uncle Sam always coming to get his money. That $10,000 isn't upfront either as you are paid weekly or bi-weekly. Divide $10,000 by 52 weeks and then consider the taxes at 20% (for a quick calculator trick, multiply the number by .8 to get the 20%) and if you are biweekly, divide the $10,000 by 26 and multiply the 20%. That is what you are adding to your net income each paycheck. For those of you excited, remember we only pulled Uncle Sam out. Based on where you live, you may lose more than the next, but that number will still be lower. You get less than $8000 over a year—just a thought when making that big purchase.

The next step is to identify and define your needs versus your wants. To do this, we will put an N or W next to the written bill name on each row. Let's see if your spreadsheet matches mine:

Monthly $4000	Bill	Quarterly	Yearly
$950	N Rent	$2,850	$11,400
$350	W Car	$1,050	$4,200
$320	W Credit Card	$960	$3,840
$300	W Personal Loan	$900	$3,600
$275	W Credit Card	$825	$3,300
$175	N Car Insurance	$525	$2,100
$120	W Cell Phone	$360	$1,440
$100	W Cable	$300	$1,200
$100	W Personal Loan	$300	$1,200
$60	N Electric	$180	$720
$55	N Gas	$165	$660
$30	N Water	$90	$360
$2,835		**$8,505**	**$34,020**

I am sure some of the N's and W's make immediate sense. However, for those that don't, let me explain. You are in debt because of some of these W's. For instance, you may need to travel to work and buy groceries, but did you need to take a loan out for the car? You can get a solid used car for $5000, and they will deliver that car to you! If they don't deliver, you can get a certified used car at a dealership for that amount, possibly a little more. The beautiful thing about used vehicles is that the warranty market is fantastic. They cover almost anything, and you pay one time for the coverage and a small deductible when you use your warranty. They have plans now that cover your tires for the life of the car! I am making a point here that the price you pay for the vehicle is not the actual amount you are paying. If you tried to sell your car chances, are it is nowhere near the amount you owe regarding its value. You typically can only keep up with your car's depreciation with a 2-year loan. The average consumer utilizes a 5-to-7-year loan. It doesn't sound as bad when they say 60 –84 months. Have you ever asked yourself why they don't state the years of the loan term, only the months? Remember you were approved for that car with your gross income, not considering how your net income would cover it.

You have no money to put down? You're driving a car that you wanted that has minimal value for what you are paying. Most cars keep the same model layout for at least five years before changing the design—just a thought. Ask yourself what do you need from your vehicle? Look, if you tried to sell your car for what it is worth, would it be enough to pay off the loan? I hope the car piece makes sense—many ways to get the car you want without digging a debt hole. Now the cell phone is an easy one. The cell phone industry is one of the most competitive indus-tries in America. It is one space where most consumers have no loyalty to a cell service provider.

In most cases, there aren't even contracts anymore. The deal they have now for your service could be tied with the phone you choose. Again, you are in debt. Ask yourself what do you need your phone to do? Maybe you want the newest model. Whatever your reasons are, you can more than likely find a phone of high quality to do what you want at a cheaper cost. You can probably find a better plan if you shop around too. They are always giving deals to new customers. I spent quite some time waiting for one of the cell phone companies to offer a deal I couldn't refuse. It was on my yearly to-do list to find a way to reduce my cell phone bill at least by 20%, if not half. I not only found a company that could reduce my cell phone bill by half, but they also gave me a free phone! Talk about that PAYtience. Remember, it costs you nothing to seek better deals and services at lower costs. Businesses are always competing for customers. Take advantage of that.

Okay, with that explanation out of the way, the last piece of this chapter will help you understand your finance team (the bill account) for managing your money. Add up your monthly payments that have N's. For the example above, that is about $1270 monthly. Now keep in mind the utilities listed as N's can fluctuate depending on where you live. Take the highest month you have had over the past year and use that as your baseline. This step may double a few of your bills, which is okay. Being prepared will pay off faster than you think. That brings the new total to $1415.

Before you turn on any auto-pay, you will first separate your paycheck into this account. This step focuses on your monthly pay frequency and the minimum needed to get started. You will divide your monthly need number by 2 or 4 to know what needs to be pulled from each check to manage your bills based on whether you receive income weekly or bi-weekly. The remainder of your income, assuming you have a direct deposit process from your job already set up, will flow into your account. The amount left will be your future disposable income. I recommend setting only a few bills at a time until you are comfortable to add the rest. If you are ready to dive in, go online to your accounts and look to move your due dates closer to when you will have the bulk of your bill amount in the account. If you are unsure where the option is, you can call your bill companies to walk you through the process or make the changes for you. If your last paycheck is the end of the month, pick the last two days of the month to give yourself some time to allow your bill account to build up your bill money. If you are bi-weekly and your last check is more of the middle of the month, the end of the third week of the month should give you enough time to build up to cover your bills. You can still pay your bills from here with the credit union routing number and your account number until you are comfortable with autopay. Remember, the purpose of setting up our needs through auto pay and separating the check allows you to focus on disposable income to get out of debt faster by concentrating just on the debt. This concept will also be vital to how you stay out of debt once you achieve your goals. Keep in mind there are checks and excess bill money we purposefully do not include so that you budget in a break from the hustle for an opportunity to celebrate.

Putting your bills on auto-pay is like having a finance team. You are still the boss and make all the decisions, but the finance team gives you peace of mind as you build up the finance team's responsibility through this process. I know some folks are not fans of auto pay since they want to control the exact amount paid at the precise time. The reality is your bills can be one less thing you worry about as you get out of this debt hole. Now we need to create a second list that reflects just the wants. This list is what we will focus on in the next chapter. On another page or tab, if using excel/google sheets, recreate the list showing only the wants with just the monthly payments and the titles for each. We will add one column here, which is the total amount owed or the total amount you have left to pay, and we will add our monthly disposable amount next to monthly so we can track any changes. See the example below:

Monthly $1020	Bill	TOTAL
$350	W Car	$18,000
$320	W Credit Card	$7,400
$300	W Personal Loan	$17,000
$275	W Credit Card	$5,000
$120	W Cell Phone	$850
$100	W Cable	0
$100	W Personal Loan	$3,400
$1,565		**$51,650**

Here is how we know what we are working with:

$4000 - Monthly Net Income

$1415 – Monthly Bills

$2585 – Disposable Income

$1565 – Wants

$1020 – What we have left to make decisions in managing life and debt

Monthly Net Income – Monthly Bills = Disposable Income (Long term goal)

Disposable Income – Wants = What we have left to manage life and debt (Short-term financial management.)

The book's examples support you for the math, and listing out your expenses can be referenced to help you build out your information. Please don't compare as everyone has a different size debt hole and net income. Understanding these examples will help you understand your current situation to begin moving forward. Please reference the grids and do the math for your finances. It will help you make the best decision on which strategy will work best for you to meet your goal! Think about the improved credit score and increased disposable income coupled with better spending habits. It is a life where you can achieve bigger goals faster and not stress about your finances. Maintaining your mindset during this process can, at times, be challenging. You will notice in any of the calculations for paying off your debt the bill account excess will not be included. It is super important that every three months, you truly take advantage of the additional money your finance team has set aside and make sure you are celebrating every three months as you continue to move mountains. Maybe you go 50/50, and half of the excess money goes to debt, and the rest you splurge on some champagne and a steak! Either way, make sure you are taking some time to celebrate your efforts and those you have a part of your journey.

Once you have everything written out for your finances based on the math provided, you must understand as we move on to the next chapter, we do not include the minimum payments as part of paying off the debt in total. Your minimum payments to your credit cards are not a part of our calculations because 99% of your debt charges an interest rate. When you pay the minimum payment monthly, most of that payment will go to the interest charged and not the principal. The principal amount is what you owe, and the interest is what you pay for owing it. The most effective way to pay your debt off is to pay more than the minimum payment. This process is the only way to understand the timeline of paying off your debt. This method also helps with your mental and emotional space. You are focusing on one goal instead of many. Don't try to do the math of how much your minimum monthly payment will go to the principal. You only focus on the additional money you send and the math for the balance owed. This strategy is by far the most effective way to understand how to reach your goal. I will share strategies in the next chapter to shorten your journey by paying off your debt. This method will keep you on track regardless of what approach you use, and I encourage you to use as many that can fit your lifestyle, mental and emotional space.

Step 2: Identify monthly reoccurring bills

Step 3: Identify wants versus needs

Step 4: Calculate the amount needed for monthly reoccurring bills

Step 5: Allocate that amount from your check based on your pay frequency through direct deposit

Step 6: Begin setting up your bills to auto-pay from your bill account

Step 7: Let the finance team work the bills so you can work the debt!

Outstanding job as you are now one step closer! Now that we have finished this chapter, some work to be done for the journey ahead! See the questions below and remember to be honest. You may keep some of these answers from everyone else, but it is essential to be upfront and honest with YOU!

- Do you need to increase your income to achieve your goals?
- How much do you take home monthly? Quarterly? Yearly?
- How much do you spend on take out?
- Do you enjoy your own cooking?
- Do you find yourself throwing out food whether it expired or was old leftovers?
- What is about pre made meals or take out you enjoy most?
- Why is someone else's name more important than your goals?
- Who is paying your debt?
- How can you make your house work for you?
- What percentage should my monthly expenses be?
- How much disposable income do you want to enjoy?
- Ask yourself what do you need from your vehicle?
- If you tried to sell your car for what it is worth would it be enough to pay off the loan?
- Ask yourself what do you need your phone to do?

4

STRATEGIES BASED ON MENTALITY & EMOTION

"Do what you have to do until you can do what you want to do."

— OPRAH WINFREY

If you haven't opened that second bill account and read this chapter, you skipped a step! Go and open a second account as we begin to move through the strategies and re-read through the last chapter if you are unsure of the steps.

DO NOT FILE BANKRUPTCY! I say this because, at a minimum, anything you want to do that requires a credit check you will be unable to accomplish for *at least seven years.*

However, there are lasting effects even after the seven years that can last up to **15 YEARS!!!** You won't be able to get a credit card, buy a car via a loan, and may not even be able to qualify to rent. The long-term impact of bankruptcy can be by far a more significant challenge to overcome than actually paying your debt down. Remember not everything that is debt is forgiven by filing for bankruptcy. Student loans, mortgages, and other items you may still be on the hook to pay for after filing for bankruptcy. I have a family member who filed for bankruptcy and had to wait for 15 years to get a credit card with a $300 limit. Your road to debt-free will already be a challenge, so no need to make it even harder thinking this would be a fix. If you genuinely feel this is your only answer, reach out to a few bankruptcy lawyers and see what they tell you. There are many details they will not cover, or they won't offer a direct answer. Read the fine print and do the math and use the spreadsheet as a tool in making your decisions. It can mean saving yourself a decade of unnecessary hardship.

At this point, you should know what you have left at the end of each month to work with as disposable income. The only item we have not factored into our budget is food. As stated, this will vary for all of you. By not factoring in the food, you eat you can start to learn the impact of your decisions. The more you spend on take-out instead of taking in your own kitchen experience, the longer you remain in debt. A take-out meal costing over $100 a few times a month makes a big difference.

As you read the paragraph of this chapter, think about where you keep the scissors, grab them along with your credit cards, and cut them up. Your credit card company will gladly send you new ones once you are ready to use them responsibly. If, for whatever reason, you do not want to cut them up, give them to a trusted relative or friend. A warning to those in fear of cutting them up, your journey may take longer due to your mental space. Part with them now and re-join them when you are ready to respect the awe of their power. Put the book down and cut the cards up before you continue reading. You can do this if you have gotten this far. I believe in you and all you are capable of doing! I will be waiting for you to return.

Cards cut up? Let's GO!!! Full disclosure here, I will list what I consider to be the most significant sacrifice down to what I think the slightest sacrifice. I am sure those who are reading this and hungry to beat this debt down are ready to go hard, sacrifice big, and be happy and debt-free in a shorter amount of time. I will list out the impact of these strategies to make the best decision possible for you. I encourage you to leverage multiple methods as they will speed up the process. To clarify what the sacrifice is, well, that's time. The essential thing in our lives is when we want to do what we want—the time we spend with our families, friends, and solitude. Unfortunately, debt can prevent us from how we want to spend our time. On another note, I will only cover strategies in this chapter to manage your debt journey, not the method in which you pay your debt off. I will cover that in another chapter as there is another list of strategies to that as well. Deciding how you pay your debt off is relatively easy; however, the approach in managing your journey lies as the actual challenge. This chapter can truly determine the amount of time spent on this journey.

First and what I believe to be the most significant sacrifice: increase your income.

Many options here, but most primarily fall on your current schedule and pay for the job you have now. If you have a job that pays overtime (OT), it will be easier for you to work as much overtime (OT) as you can. If you are an employee paid salary chances, are you will have to get a second job which would also be the case if you are considered an hourly employee and your job does not offer overtime (OT). If you can commit to at least 20 hours a week, you will find you can bring home a net income from a second job equalling at least $1000 at the end of the month after Uncle Sam comes. If you can crank out 80 hours a week between 2 full-time jobs, you can get $2000 at the end of the month. Here is some advice to those who have the ambition to work two full-time jobs. Working 80-hour weeks is hard on your mind and body, and you will have to care for them differently than you normally would when picking up extra hours at your current job or a second part-time job. The higher in age, the tougher on the body. That does not mean you can't knock it out of the park. It means you have to make some small changes to your diet. Plant-based or Keto will get you the energy and work to heal your body faster. I prefer plant-based, personally, as I have tried both and found better results with plant-based. Since I was also short on time working 80 hours a week, I transitioned to a smoothie diet. The only day I overate was my first day off from my primary job. I would switch between the plant-based and backyard barbecue on my only one day to myself. That was my personal decision. If you take the plant-based smoothie route, which I felt took the shortest time to prepare and consume, giving me more time to rest, add a tablespoon of turmeric to support the body in its healing after you have completed your day of work. My daily consumption was two huge smoothies with the following ingredients: 1 banana, 1 avocado, 1 cup of spinach, 1 cup of kale, 1 cup of mixed berries, 1 cup of coconut milk, 1 tsp of powdered sea moss bladder whack, and 1 tablespoon of turmeric. This combination will not only fill you up but give you plenty of energy to keep you moving and keep your body strong. I ate fruits and vegetables in between smoothies to keep my energy flowing. Now, if you are on a smoothie diet, chances are your family didn't switch over with you. Creating a weekly menu and using your $10 meals will make a huge difference. It will be an activity your family looks forward to while you put in extra hours. Making your family's favorites from scratch will go a long way with them and your bank account. Working 80 hours a week isn't easy. I mentioned the advantage of creating a menu with your family. The menu can contribute to your time to rest and provide a clear direction while putting in a lot of extra hours. It will be what you look forward to, whether you or your partner is preparing the meal. Even if it's not your partner, in practicing humility, you can gain support from those who are supporting you through your journey and see if they can take turns owning some of your menus. If you take on this challenge of an additional job, make sure it is as close to home as possible, no more than a 30-minute commute and if possible, find a company looking for temporary support as this will more than likely not be a place you stay too long. I recommend no more than three months of 80 hours. If you perform well, you can usually reduce your hours to stay on and increase your hours when you are ready to jump back in. If you remember the balances of what we owe to our wants, you may think this isn't worth it, but the reality is three months, or less of this can support you in paying off a balance and removing it altogether from the list. Like I said, depending on how deep your debt hole is, this will take time, and making this a rotation in your life will dramatically reduce the amount of time you are paying off your debt. This step is a temporary sacrifice. With the way our world has changed recently, you may not even need to leave your home with virtual opportunities popping up everywhere. I have friends that have gotten part-time jobs they enjoyed so much they not only paid off their debt but they still work them until this day! The next piece of increasing your pay is what hourly rate is worth it? You are lucky to find a second job that does not compete with your primary one for anything over $15 an hour. If you find it, scoop it up quickly! Anything $12 - $15 an hour will get you close, if not at $1000 a month part-time and $2000 a month full-time. If the hourly rate isn't for you, look at possibly contracting yourself out to deliver food, leverage your skills on sites like fiverr.com or upwork.com for additional money. If you have confidence in learning a new skill, you can make money, work through the learning curve, and give it your best. Learning a new skill will be a long-term gain, so nothing to lose by learning. The only downside to contracting your skills out is you probably won't have consistent income, but that doesn't mean it isn't worth trying. If you are confident in your skills, you can see a big lift here in a shorter amount of time if you offer quality service with your skills. Last but not least, for this heavy sacrifice is you may feel you don't have the time to do it either because of responsibilities you already have. It may be children or other relatives that may rely on you for support. This opportunity is where we will first practice humility. You can choose to have people join you on your journey to grow with and appreciate, or you can go it alone. Depending on your responsibilities, it's time you made a few phone calls or a few visits. I stated earlier this would have taken me much longer without my sister. She came through for me and helped me maximize my time and dollar when it came to my food budget. Using her box store discount card, I reduced my food budget by 20%. She also happens to be a phenomenal cook. I was glad to take her leftovers as this covered my time and taste buds on my days off. It was wholesome, helpful and it made our relationship even stronger. Not only did my sister support me through her cooking and discount card, but a close friend would also come to feed me as well and remind me that I was almost there and I could do it. That close friend kept me moving when I thought I would give up. That same close friend, a mother of 2 boys, one toddler, and one teenager, also sought to increase her income. Her strategy of practicing humility she contacted a few relatives and friends to ask that they commit to one day a week to watch her children so she can work late into the night. By doing this, her children got to spend more time and create stronger bonds with their aunt, grandfather, and me, as I was all too happy to pay back the support she had given me. By asking more than one person, she aimed not to burden anyone.

Once you get over the physical piece transitioning to the smoothies and living in super comfortable running shoes, the mental part creeps up. Do you start asking yourself why I am doing this? Do I need to do THIS? It's tough, but if you focus on finding love in what you are doing and that pot of gold on the other side of the debt hole, it can be a breeze. Having a connection with someone who will be your cheerleader helps more than you think. It's not just about the relatives and friends who will help you out. It's about the kids too. Think about how your children would feel spending more time with a relative who they love and enjoy. Yes, you may be spending less time with them, but they are in the hands of someone you chose, and it's not forever, only a few months at a time, depending on how you make your decisions. For those who expand on current relationships, challenge yourself and achieve your goal faster – go and move mountains! The example below of what our decision in managing life and debt, the money coupled with a second job be it full-time or part-time over three months and let's say those first three months you are spending half of your disposable income on food:

	Month 1	Month 2	Month 3
Full time/OT	$2,000	$4,000	$6,000
Part time/OT	$1,000	$2,000	$3,000
No 2nd job/OT	$510	$1,020	$1,530

Monthly $1020	Bill	TOTAL
$350	W Car	$18,000
$320	W Credit Card	$7,400
$300	W Personal Loan	$17,000
$275	W Credit Card	$5,000
$120	W Cell Phone	$850
$100	W Cable	0
$100	W Personal Loan	$3,400
$1,565		**$51,650**

Doing the math here by working a 2nd full-time job, we would have been able to pay off a few items or at the very least one more significant item. The $6000 + $1530 = $7530, which would have reduced one of your debts off the board. The strategy in how we pay items off will be listed later on in another chapter. Again, it will correlate with your mental and emotional space to help you make a decision. Even working a part-time job, you would have been able to reduce another want. This strategy is the power when you increase your income. Keep in mind this increase is temporary and strictly focused on paying off your debt. It will take a solid mental and emotional state to achieve this, and it will be the most rewarding. Keep in mind each debt you remove here improves your credit score and reduces the time of your journey.

Second most significant sacrifice: Renting part of your living space.

For the homeowner, this may not be what you dreamed of when you first bought your home, and to the renter, you are probably thinking how? Well, depending on the size of your home and the location, you might be able to receive $500 - $1000+ monthly. I am sure you have heard of Airbnb, and guess what? Travelers love to use it even if it is for a private bedroom and you share the bathroom. It's the second biggest sacrifice because your home may be a space you are not comfortable sharing with strangers. This option is why I stated homeowners have more opportunities to play with here as they may have a separate entrance to the home. If you have a finished basement with a full bathroom, pop a hot plate and a microwave down there, lock the basement door, and you might even be able to rent it out monthly. Most townships or counties do not require any licensing or certification if you rent part of your primary residence. Do you have a garage? Rent it out for storage. Again quite a few options here, but it depends on how comfortable you are sharing your space. See what the rental rates are in your area, only compare to what you can similarly offer, and boom increased income. It may be smaller than the additional job, but everything helps. If you are doing both, you can dramatically shorten your journey. I am sure some of you are reading this have already put the book down and started your search on Airbnb, while others have already made up their mind and are not sharing an inch of their home. Being honest with yourself is crucial, and if this is something you are not comfortable with, good for you. You don't have to use every strategy given. Your mental and emotional space is essential, and you recognizing that is important too. Specifically for the renters, you can start to plan and prepare when your lease is up to move in with a relative or close friend to have more money to send towards your debt instead of renting. Always coordinate what will be needed to be contributed monthly for your new space and how you can help around the house. Setting expectations upfront can help avoid any misunderstandings in the future.

Third most significant sacrifice: Your daily spending habits on wants.

People make small purchases daily, such as coffee in the morning, a take-out meal at lunch, or maybe a few scratch-offs throughout the week. Many of these habits are typically harmless and help you through your daily routine. They may be moments you look forward to each day. If a cup of coffee costs you one dollar five days a week, it's probably not going to give you a big boost at the end of the month, but if you are spending

$5 or more dollars 5 days a week on coffee, you might want to look at how you can cut the cost. This daily routine is a sacrifice that can impact your mental and emotional space as it may be something you look forward to experiencing each day. Some apps can track your daily spending habits, but you can also write down what you are spending daily or weekly to see the impact and look to cut there. Anything $100 or more is something you want to reduce. If you can cut it out completely, it will speed up your journey. I had a nasty habit of smoking a pack a day. Not only was it tough on my lungs it was pretty expensive. Where I live, cigarettes are $10 a pack, which adds up to $300 monthly. I started making my own cigarettes at half the price of what I was paying and lasted twice as long. I ultimately switched over to vaping. The savings I saw every month was blowing my mind, and I haven't smoked a cigarette since. You may not be a smoker, but you are bleeding money from your pocket some-where. Find a lower-cost supplement, whether you are doing it yourself or just choosing a lower-cost option. Remember, you aren't giving it up for good. You are explicitly focusing on getting out of debt.

Last but not least – consolidation.

You may think going to get a loan to consolidate everything is easy, but, in my experience, I have found a lot of people have a fear of going to their local bank or credit union to see what options they have. Being turned down is disappointing, but if you don't know your options, you won't see what you could benefit from learning about loan consolidation. I spent almost a year drowning in debt, and every time I saw a commercial about consolidation, I always thought it was another scam. I ultimately learned that although some, not all of the consolidation companies out there are scamming you. However, they may not be able to solve everything. One of the more significant downsides with consolidation companies is that most require you to cancel or close your credit cards. If this sounds like a good idea, you still have a lot to learn about credit scores. I cover this in more detail later on in this book but know that this can extend your journey farther out than expected. After talking to my sister about the idea of refinancing, I realized I could try to refinance some of W's at my local credit union. The worst that could happen was nothing, as being declined means you are in the same place you were when you walked through the door. If approved, you could drastically change your journey's length of time, and the best part is the process costs you nothing. I went down and filled out the paperwork, and boom!

Not only was I approved, since the interest rates at a credit union are lower compared to the other interest rates, I automatically gained more money for my disposable income. With the interest rate now lower, my overall W's monthly payments dropped by more than 20%, and my previous loans had a year taken off just through the interest alone. The cost reduction meant I increased the monthly money to use towards paying off my debt and shortened the process simultaneously. Now, this was fantastic news and something to keep in mind. Your credit union will weigh more heavily on the ability you have to repay the loan than a bank. A bank will focus more on your credit score. Although the credit union considers it, they also consider longevity at a job and home. You have a higher probability of being approved even if your credit is not the best. The other excellent option with a credit union is to receive a personal loan at a lower interest rate than you would receive at a bank. You can't refinance your credit card like you can a car, but you can take out a personal loan to pay off a balance. Even if you can't qualify for all of the credit cards you have, using this can cut down on the payment and length of time. You can truly gain some leverage here, so give it a shot, work with your credit union and see what your options are. You lose nothing by trying! I have a close relative that did not want to increase their income or rent out their space and decided to use the consolidation option. They calculated all of their minimum payments together to find out what they could afford as a monthly payment to understand which term or length of time for the loan would work best. The more you can pay, the shorter your loan duration will be. The less you can pay, the longer the term of the loan. While working with their credit union, they could find a 3-year loan. They could have selected a 5-year loan, but by calculating what they were already paying and not trying to have additional money now, they know in 3 years, everything is 100% ultimately paid for in full. They also send extra money every three months to shorten the time. There are options for everyone, and more than likely, your credit union or a good bank will not require you to cancel your credit cards, helping you keep the depth of history needed for your credit score.

This information, coupled with everything listed above, is a recipe to assist in paying off your debt in record timing. There are a few downsides when you add in consolidation companies. Remember when you chose not to cut up that credit card? Gave it to a friend or family member? When using the consolidation method, those who kept the credit cards accessible are more than likely going to use them and create more debt. Consolidation is nice because all of your loans and credit cards go into one payment, and it will usually provide some breathing room, adding to the amount of money you can spend since it is all now locked in at a lower interest rate. If you take this route, you must understand what can happen and avoid it at all costs, cut up the credit cards. Depending on who you are using, they may have a requirement where you have to close your credit card account. Credit unions won't require that, but debt consolidation companies might. Your credit score isn't only paying your bills on time but also the length of history. Once you close that card, you lose that history. Those black eyes of missed payments don't stay on there forever, and you can redeem yourself by improving your credit score by making payments on time. I have a credit card I got at 19 and will never part with it simply because it is part of why my credit score is so high. It was my first, and although I rarely use it today, it keeps my credit solid. I had some black eyes when I first received it, but that is all water under the bridge. Most credit card companies are looking at the last 18 months – 2 years of payment history. The depth of history, though, is essential. If working with a debt consolidation company, weigh the outcome if you have to close your credit cards. Yes, you may save some money, but what will you have to do to get that level of history back to when building your credit score. You can't go back in time and open up a credit card so keep this in mind if this is what they offer when using a debt consolidation company. One journey shouldn't cause you to create a new one to now build credit. If you don't believe me, ask them, and their response will tell it all. I like the credit union option better as they aren't trying to sell you anything, whereas a debt consolidation company is. Not saying you shouldn't use it. Be smart with how it will impact your overall goal. Be careful of fees and read the fine print. You have the tools now to help you with the math, so don't get caught signing up for a bad deal.

I hope that by the end of this chapter, you are deciding what your mental and emotional space can handle. We covered a lot, and you should hopefully be getting ready to make that move. If, for whatever reason, none of the strategies work for you, check your answers from the first chapter and think about why you provided those answers. It's all fun and games until you have to face what's right in front of you. The longer you ignore it, the harder it is to overcome. I am not a fan of bankruptcy, and it is something I plan never to have to experience, and I hope anyone reading this never has to go through it either.

Remember to look at your answers from the first chapter for the questions below.

- Have you been able to admit to yourself how you feel about your current reality?
- What are you willing to do to get out of debt?
- How quickly do you want your reality to change?

5

MINIMUM PAYMENT OR THE INTEREST RATE?

"You always have two choices: your commitment versus your fear."

— SAMMY DAVIS JR.

We will cover a few scenarios that will show the different options and mindset behind chasing the minimum payment or the interest rate. Based on some of the decisions you made from the last chapter, the interest and the monthly minimum amount may not be of concern as you have chosen to consolidate all of your debt into one payment with a locked-in interest rate. If you decided to refinance a few of your wants at the credit union, you might have consolidated some but not all of your W's. If you tried and didn't qualify for either, there is still plenty of options, and you will move that mountain of debt and climb out of that hole forever.

When structuring your strategy, you must note that you do not change the monthly payment as you begin this process. If you can commit to that monthly payment, you can commit to sending that same amount to another debt. Do not give in to comfort from your monthly payments reducing as your total owed reduces. Credit cards will reduce the minimum amount the more you pay off your total balance. I have a whole chapter dedicated to not losing your mind and thinking you have to give it all up to get out of debt. Maintaining the minimum payment allows you to know what you can part with when paid to pay off more debt immediately. I will provide examples of how to map it out as we go through the different paying-off debt strategies.

If you have credit card debt, you want to start there. Your credit card will typically be your highest in payment and interest. It would help if you could refinance the car lowering your interest rate and lowering your cost. This scenario puts us right in the credit card space. If you are not familiar with how your credit card charges you interest, I encourage you to read your statement and look at the APR, the annual percentage rate. This annual percentage rate is the first place your credit card gets you as most credit cards charge you a daily percentage which is why this is the first that needs to go. Because of the daily interest charge, you will have to continually update the total balance after paying on your credit card. The more frequently you can pay, the faster you can pay it off. Remember the example from the previous chapter with what you could accomplish in 3 months with a 2nd full-time job:

	Month 1	Month 2	Month 3
Full time/OT	$2,000	$4,000	$6,000
Part time/OT	$1,000	$2,000	$3,000
No 2nd job/OT	$510	$1,020	$1,530

Monthly $1020	**Bill**	**TOTAL**
$350	W Car	$18,000
$320	W Credit Card	$7,400
$300	W Personal Loan	$17,000
$275	W Credit Card	$5,000
$120	W Cell Phone	$850
$100	W Cable	0
$100	W Personal Loan	$3,400
$1,565		**$51,650**

Because I want to encourage those reading this book who may be unable to take advantage of any refinancing or debt consolidation, my examples will reflect no impact from that strategy. Those of you who could benefit from that strategy update your numbers on your sheet, still follow along, and remember your journey just got shorter!

If we add the first month, the money we have after buying food for the month plus we made $2000 from our 2nd full-time job gives us a total of $2510 that we could send to our credit card.

Since we don't send it all at once, we reduce the credit card's amount charged in interest, thus lowering our monthly payment and balance for the next month. Every time you carry a balance into the next month, the credit card company will charge you for doing so daily. If you receive income weekly or bi-weekly, every check, you receive, a portion should pay off the credit card to reduce the monthly payment and the amount the credit card charges as interest. If you were to focus on any other item to pay off, you would see this would have the slightest improvement when paying the minimum payment on your credit card, which is why it is so important to pay off. You can have good credit and still have a high APR on your credit card. Get those knocked out first, and the rest are easy as you will free up a good portion of your money to work with and focus on other debts. The credit cards combined in the above example are a third out of the W's cost, which is crazy since they are 2 out of the seven items listed. If your sheet is similar to the above, you can see why you must focus on the credit cards first before you look for any other strategy to use in how you pay off your debt. Imagine you focus on the personal loan first and continue to pay your credit cards' minimums.

For, say, six months, you could have almost half the personal loan paid off but will still have a high monthly payment and balance for the credit cards. Don't waste your money. Keep it strategic and working hard for you. If you don't believe me, look at your last two credit card bills and do the math. What was the balance for both statements, and what was the minimum payment you made? The difference between the two bills will not be your payment because the credit card company will take their interest. Scary and legal how much it costs to borrow someone else's money through a piece of plastic.

By month 3, we have paid off our credit card with a balance of $7400. Congratulations!!! Yes, in 3 months, just by increasing your income, you have already crossed out a W, and good for you. You feel great now that you have accomplished something and are ready for more. Although you are just starting, it is time to celebrate! Check-in with your finance team and see how you want to use the excess money. Here is a tip along the way can help keep you focused on the game. Put a piece of paper, or you can visit your local dollar store and get a dry erase board and place one at the door you use most to leave home and another on your refrigerator. Start with the total amount you are focusing on at the top of the page, in this case, $7400. Every time you make a payment, cross that number out, and below it, write in the amount you sent and the new balance. Depending on your pay frequency, this may be a weekly activity that you will begin to look forward to as you track your progress. When I embarked on this journey on my last debt run, my primary job paid me bi-weekly, and my 2nd full-time job paid me weekly. Nothing more excited me than the day before receiving my pay. I barely needed sleep as the adrenaline of knowing how much closer I was that day than the week before kept me moving. We will review timelines in another chapter to help you make your decisions and understand the impact of your sacrifice. Now to update our spreadsheet with that credit card off the list:

Monthly $1340	Bill	TOTAL
$350	W Car	$18,000
~~$320~~	~~W Credit Card~~	~~$7,400~~
$300	W Personal Loan	$17,000
$275	W Credit Card	$5,000
$120	W Cell Phone	$850
$100	W Cable	0
$100	W Personal Loan	$3,400
$1,245		**$44,250**

Remember that $1020 is what we have left to make decisions in managing life and debt. Now that we have paid off that credit card, we have increased this number to $1340. One credit card to go, and you can now make different decisions that will have an impact. Remember the finance team-managed account? Your finance team should have been able to provide you some extra cash if you have committed to not touching anything additional during the three months. Now you can see the amount you have over what you need to have and decide to use it towards debt, celebrating, or saving. Your finance team helped you stay focused on the goal, not having to think about bills while also setting aside money for you to use as you see fit. Consider it your quarterly bonus for a job well done. For months 4-6, you decided you like the job and will keep it part-time for the next three months while continuing to determine your next move to reduce your debt. The process just reviewed is what this looks like below on paper:

	Month 4	Month 5	Month 6
Full time/OT	$2,000	$4,000	$6,000
Part time/OT	$1,000	$2,000	$3,000
No 2nd job/OT	$830	$1,660	$2,490

By month 6, you have been able to pay off both credit cards! Part-time plus no 2nd job gives you $5490. Celebrate! That minimum payment from the previous credit card moved the needle here. Adding to your disposable income with the minimum amount of the debt recently paid off is the power the additional income can bring even if you are not approved to use other financing options. Now imagine if you could work, rent your space out and consolidate some of your finances. You would be much farther in your goal within six months than you would have ever believed. Combining these strategies is a winning recipe to get out of debt quickly. I hope this helps you see that you can cover a lot of roads on your journey by using multiple strategies. Just do the math, and you can see the bene-fit. With both credit cards paid off, you can breathe a little better and more than likely take another visit to the bank and see what your options are now that you have paid off the credit cards.

Monthly $1615	Bill	TOTAL
$350	W Car	$18,000
~~$320~~	~~W Credit Card~~	~~$7,400~~
$300	W Personal Loan	$17,000
~~$275~~	~~W Credit Card~~	~~$5,000~~
$120	W Cell Phone	$850
$100	W Cable	0
$100	W Personal Loan	$3,400
$970		**$39,250**

We now have $1615 left to make decisions in managing life and debt. Best six months ever! You challenged yourself and grew your bond with family and friends, and you are closer to your goal than ever before. Celebrate the two wins but remember you still have a list to tackle and a plan to reach. The good thing is for the six months; you realize while you reduced your take-out, you were still wasting food and were able to shave back on what you were spending. Nice work! When we started, we were only able to put up $510 of our monthly net income to pay off our debt. Now that we have paid a few items off and have learned some lessons, we can comfortably commit to $1230 monthly to paying off debt. This part of the process is where you can begin to make decisive decisions.

If you have ever taken a steep hike, you know that the bottom is rough. As you get to the top, it begins to feel short, effortless, and rewarding. There is no thought of the hike back down as you have made it to the top of the mountain. When you make a snowball, you will notice by rolling a smaller one in the snow; you can get a big one pretty quickly. These are the two most popular methods in paying off debt: the snowball effect and the climb. With the snowball effect, you focus on paying off the debt with the lowest minimum payment. You have to add that minimum payment to the next debt up on the list and increase the amount you can pay towards your debt over time. The climb you start in the opposite direction paying the highest minimum payment to increase the amount you can pay towards your debt over time. Both have the same goal, just different approaches. You can use both methods, the snowball and the climb with interest rates. Now that your credit cards are out of the debt hole, interest rates are generally not as impactful on loans. If you can follow a timeline that can pay off a loan in under 12 months chances, are you will not see a significant benefit. If you have an interest over 14% that charges daily interest on the loan instead of monthly, it will be similar to the credit card, and you probably want to pay that off first. If you are at this point with no credit card debt, it is improbable you are not approved for any refinance options or a lower interest loan to pay off a loan at a higher interest rate, so keep in mind that is something to be accomplished at this stage.

In the doubtful chance, you again did not qualify for any options at the credit union decide next your course of action for the snowball or the climb. Although I am not a fan of the banks, a good bank might be able to support you with refinancing or consolidation, so shop around and keep the interest rate at the top of your mind when looking for who can provide the best offer. Here are the mental and emotional impacts of both methods. The snowball method is popular as it supports the microwave society we live in as you can accomplish paying items off quickly. Just looking at the chart of W's within two months without working a part-time or 2nd full-time job, you could easily knock out two or more items and remove them from the list. That sounds awesome now, but your gain from that would probably be $120-$140 additional dollars to add to paying off your debt. You still have two big bills to get through, and you may not have the patience to continue to sacrifice that much longer. I always recommend temporary sacrifices as the longer they take, the more it can drain you mentally and emotionally. This check-in is where being honest with yourself is crucial as you do not want to decide to dig the debt hole any deeper. You still have some options along the way to increase the amount you can send to paying off your debt but under-standing your goal is what will keep you honest. The snowball strategy is suitable for anyone undedicated to getting out of debt quickly. Some will be comfortable with simply letting the rest of their debt play out, still sending additional money but probably not as much to get out of debt quickly. Remember those questions I asked in the beginning and at the end of the last chapter. We will review them again at the end of this chapter as well.

Now the climb works well if you are still hungry to make a dent in your debt. Leverage that energy now so you can finish your journey quickly. By focusing on your most enormous debt first, it will take longer to pay off just one debt, but once you cross the finish line for the biggest one, your journey gets more manageable and shorter. This method is challenging mentally and emotionally as this could be the longest part of your trip on becoming debt-free. You are six months in, and you may ask can you do another six months of sacrifice? Again, all up to you and how you manage your journey. As you will notice, a tip before we begin, the car should now be our most significant payment and total debt. I would never recommend paying your vehicle off unless you pass it on to your kids or a family member, meaning if there is no long-term desire to keep it, your goal should be how you can use it to benefit you. If you have a car, you more than likely need it based on where you live and your lifestyle, consider the following options. Search the value of your vehicle and compare it to others as far as mileage and cleanliness listed by other owners, not dealerships. After reviewing a few cars, the exact year, make and model as yours, you will have an idea of what your vehicle is worth. You can also use Kelley Blue Book to help you understand the value your car currently has based on you personally selling it or trading it in. Let's say our car is worth $14,000. To get out of this debt, we don't need to pay $18,000, but only half of that. Here's why first you need to at least get the car to what it is worth and quickly as most vehicles depreciate every year. Second, I mentioned in Chapter 3: Understanding Your Expenses versus Income that you can get a solid car for $5000, and they might even deliver it to you.

$18,000-$14,000=$4000, $4000+$5000=$9000

By paying your car loan down by $9000 in less than a year, you can get yourself out of this monthly expense and own a car outright. This process would also reduce your insurance since you own the vehicle. There are specific requirements you would no longer need to have through your insurance. Now, this is 100% up to you and what your plans are with your vehicle. If you are still hungry month 6-9, pick up that second job, and let's, see the outcome:

	Month 7	Month 8	Month 9
Full time/OT	$2,000	$4,000	$6,000
Part time/OT	$1,000	$2,000	$3,000
No 2nd job/OT	$1,230	$2,460	$3,690

With a full-time income, you can pay off enough of the car loan to sell the car, pay off the remainder of the loan, and have enough money left over to purchase a vehicle. The full-time job over three months gives you $6000 in net income, and your primary check and improvement in your removal of credit card debt give you $3690, which equals $9690 total. In 3 months, you would be able to cross the most expensive item off of your list. In 9 months, you have paid off more than half your debt, increasing your disposable income. If you choose to keep the car long-term based on your plans, pay the minimum and chase another bill. Remember the interest you are paying on the loan of your car. Each time you pay off a debt, I encourage you to go back to the credit union to try and refinance that loan at a better interest rate until you are approved. Once you are approved, you know you are paying the least in interest and can pay it off sooner as you pay the payments. It will save you thousands in the long run. Hopefully, this shows the impact of credit card debt, and a car loan can drastically improve your financial stability. More importantly, your overall bills have gone down across the board. You by now should have achieved your monthly expenses under 50% of your net income monthly.

Monthly $1965	Bill	TOTAL
~~$350~~	~~W Car~~	~~$18,000~~
~~$320~~	~~W Credit Card~~	~~$7,400~~
$300	W Personal Loan	$17,000
~~$275~~	~~W Credit Card~~	~~$5,000~~
$120	W Cell Phone	$850
$100	W Cable	0
$100	W Personal Loan	$3,400
$620		**$21,250**

Monthly	Bill	Quarterly	Yearly
$950	N Rent	$2,850	$11,400
~~$350~~	~~W Car~~	~~$1,050~~	~~$4,200~~
~~$320~~	~~W Credit Card~~	~~$960~~	~~$3,840~~
$300	W Personal Loan	$900	$3,600
~~$275~~	~~W Credit Card~~	~~$825~~	~~$3,300~~
$140	N Car Insurance	$420	$1,680
$120	W Cell Phone	$360	$1,440
$100	W Cable	$300	$1,200
$100	W Personal Loan	$300	$1,200
$60	N Electric	$180	$720
$55	N Gas	$165	$660
$30	N Water	$90	$360
$1,855		**$5,565**	**$22,260**

We are now left with three total debt items to focus on paying off. You have accomplished a lot in 9 months. Celebrate! Check your bill account and decide how you want to spend what your finance team has set aside for you. You can use it to pay off more debt, spend it or save it. It's your quarterly bonus. Now all that is left is the two personal loans and the remaining balance owed for your cell phone. You have $1600 a month to focus on paying off your debt.

Snowball method:

You go back part-time or started renting your space as you have become more comfortable now with the idea of increasing the amount you can commit to paying off your debt.

- Month 10 – Cell Phone-Paid in total, bringing your cell phone bill down and money left over to pay the smaller personal loan.
- Month 11 – Smaller Personal Loan paid in full with money left over to start paying the last loan and snowballing the amount of money to pay off your debt sooner.
- Month 12 – Only one loan is left to pay off, and you bring the balance down to $10,655.

Example below:

	Month 10	Month 11	Month 12
Full time/OT	$2,000	$4,000	$6,000
Part time/OT W/Rent	$1,500	$3,000	$4,500
No 2nd job/OT	$1,600	$3,200	$4,800

	Total	Month 10	Month 11	Month 12
Cell Phone	$850	$850-$3,100	0	0
Personal Loan	$3,400	$3,400-$2,250	$1,150-$3,100	0
Personal Loan	$17,000		$17,000 -$1,950	$15,050 -$3,100

In a year, Kudos to you, getting your debt down to just one last loan! It was an arduous journey, but you accomplished it. This result is what the snowball method looks like had you chosen that method now with $11,950 left to pay. From experience, both personal and others who have taken the journey, people tend to get comfortable, and it then takes years to pay off this last loan and possibly begin to dig the debt hole deeper. The ambition to reach your goal keeps you hungry and willing to accomplish more in a short amount of time. The snowball method creates comfort in your mental and emotional space. Remember what you set out to achieve and finish through. If this was your goal, great if not, remember the previous chapters' questions and review with yourself and your cheerleader.

Climb method:

You went back full time and started renting your space as you have become more comfortable now with the idea of increasing the amount you can commit to paying off your debt.

- Month 1 - $4,100 paid to the largest loan balance. New balance $12,900.
- Month 2 - $4,475 paid to the largest loan balance. New balance $8,800.
- Month 3 - $4,475 paid to the largest loan balance. New balance $4,700.

Example below:

	Month 10	Month 11	Month 12
Full time/OT W/Rent	$2,500	$5,000	$7,500
Part time/OT W/Rent	$1,500	$3,000	$4,500
No 2nd job/OT	$1,600	$3,200	$4,800

	Total	Month 10	Month 11	Month 12
		$17,000	$12,900	$8,800
Personal Loan	$17,000	-$4,100	-$4,100	-$4,100
Personal Loan	$3,400	0	0	0
Cell Phone	$850	0	0	0

Congratulations, you now have under $10,000 left to pay! Celebrate! Amazing what you can accomplish in a year. The climb, although we didn't pay anything off for three months, reduced our overall debt and had a very short road left. Looking at these number's you may not want to take a break from the full-time job and give it one last month and then quit. This climb method is the power behind your mental and emotional space. You probably only need another month to finish off this loan. After that, the two items you have left can be paid in under three months even if you quit the second job. I have found that this method motivates you to do more as you can see the light at the end of the tunnel brighter and faster. Once you hit this point, there isn't comfort but celebration and satisfaction knowing you are right around the corner to check a few more boxes.

Both methods work and can improve your overall outcome and journey. It is up to you to decide what your journey looks like and how you will achieve your goal in the end. I would think after an entire year, you have had a pay raise at your primary job, and with the increase in your disposable income, you realize you can do more than you could before. We have made it to month 12! Remember to look at what your finance team has set aside for you in your bill account. The finance team has worked for you while focusing on your debt. This money set aside is your bonus to either pay towards your debt, spend or save. When I structured my bills in this format, I chose to use the money for my debt, and it cut months off my process. Once I saw the amount in there, I didn't have to plan for future savings. Once I paid off the debt, I just stuck to the method. Once I reached my savings amount, I started to put everything extra into my home and travel. Whenever I need to tap on my savings, I know it can replenish relatively quickly where I don't have to learn how to save and stress about bills. My finance team takes care of that. I build out my personal goals at the beginning of the year and check that account quarterly to ensure I am honest with my decisions.

One thing I have been waiting to talk about is your extra checks. If you get paid biweekly, you receive two, and if you get paid weekly, you receive 4 per year. These are checks we do not include in any of our calculations. It is essential to understand that getting out of debt can be a challenging journey, and anytime you can build a solid structure around doing more with less, the more is incredibly rewarding! Use these extra checks as you see fit. Whether you use them towards debt, used for a big night out on the town with your family, or set aside for another purpose, you didn't include them, so how you use them does not negatively impact you or your finance team.

After reading this chapter, if you say to yourself, "This can't work for me" or "This isn't possible," then you are right. If you believe paying off your debt can't be done this quickly, you won't put effort into doing it. It is super easy to get into debt but a rough road to get out quickly. Those that see how becoming debt-free with these methods and strategies will achieve success in record time. There were many times when I said I couldn't do this, and as I learned more and tried more methods, I realized I was only letting myself down by not giving it a shot. I had mental and emotional support along the way that helped increase my confidence in myself and what I could do. Now keep in mind how the scenarios were listed out. I kept these examples simple so you could follow along to understand the strategy and the math behind it. Understanding the math helps you in making your decisions. If you are spending $1 on coffee a day, you probably don't need to cut that habit as it won't produce many results. A penny saved is a penny earned, but if you love your coffee, get it at a reasonable price, look forward to it daily, and then enjoy it.

There is a reason why I say only think of things as temporary. Nothing listed here you have to do forever, and remember, the more you are willing to do, the faster you can be done with it. I have seen people leverage every strategy here and get out of debt in less than six months working straight through only focused on their goal. I encourage you to go back to the credit union as you pay off your debt if declined to refinance the loans before. They can offer rates on loans under 10%, sometimes as low as 5% - 7%, which is enormous if you have loans charging you over 10%. Most of you who read this have a high proba-bility of getting at least some of your loans refinanced at a better interest rate saving you thousands over time. If nothing else, at least attempt that. You can do so many things, and I genuinely hope you take action now to improve your financial stability and disposable income. Remember the lessons learned and never allow yourself to get back to this space. You can change your current economic status in less than 18 months but know that it will come with a temporary sacrifice.

Once you have completely paid off your debt, your mortgage or school loan will be the last item, or if you are renting, you might start to save for a home. Remember the budget method of N's and W's and how it can support your decisions. If you have a mortgage, you increased your disposable income, and now you can increase how much you are sending. You can start small and work your way up. Start with $100 and remember to review what your finance team offers every quarter. You may look at your bill account one month and decide it goes to the mortgage to cut down on the interest. If you are renting, a good rule of thumb is to have 10% of the purchase price as cash for the down payment and closing costs. Your credit union is there to show you your options. FHA loans, you only need 3.5% to put as a down payment, where other options require 5% to put as a down payment. Anyone can take advantage of the FHA loan. That 10% will help ensure you have the money necessary to cover your down payment and closing costs. There are also several state programs dedicated to first-time home buyers. Dedicate some time to seeing what you can take advantage of to reduce the overall amount you will need to purchase your home.

PAYience pays off, don't forget these lessons and enjoy a financially stable life! Your credit score should have improved, and you can now see how well you have grown by reordering one credit card at a time. The one with the lowest limit is the first one you can put back in your wallet. Please do your best not to use it for unnecessary purchases. I use mine strictly for gas and travel. If you can have three months of not using your credit card on anything extreme, continue to complete your reunion with your remaining credit cards. Make sure that you never max out your limit as you are using your credit card. When your utilization is over 30%, it will negatively impact your credit score, bringing it down. To explain further, if you have a credit card limit of $1000 and you carry a balance over $300, which is 30% of your limit, your credit score will go down.

Credit card companies don't tell you this, so make sure you know your utilization number for your credit limit. Take the limit and multiply it by 30% or .3, and this will give you the number you can carry over without impacting your credit score. I highly recommend against carrying over a balance as this can get you back into debt quickly. If you are going to use your credit card, make sure you can always pay off the balance. Think of it as a mini loan with a 30-day deadline. If it is an unnecessary purchase, ask yourself two questions. If the answer is no twice, **<u>do not make the purchase!</u>**

1. Can I ultimately pay this balance off by my due date?
2. Can I eventually pay the balance off within two months paying half by my due date?

Congratulations on getting this far! Still some strategies to help you along the way and a friendly reminder to help you through. Please review the questions below and compare them to the first and third chapters.

- Have you been able to admit to yourself how you feel about your current reality?
- What are you willing to do to get out of debt?
- How quickly do you want your reality to change?
- Ask yourself what do you need from your vehicle?

6

DO I CUT BACK?

"Beware of little expenses. A small leak will sink a great ship."

— BENJAMIN FRANKLIN

Cutting back on your expenses is not hard to do, but it can be slightly time-consuming. You have to take time to shop around for the best deal and best situation to fit your lifestyle and needs. Here is where you can maximize your dollar to help you reach your goal, and this is where you may start to make some of your temporary choices permanent. Let's look at our overall expenses:

Monthly $1020	Bill	Quarterly	Yearly
$950	N Rent	$2,850	$11,400
$350	W Car	$1,050	$4,200
$320	W Credit Card	$960	$3,840
$300	W Personal Loan	$900	$3,600
$275	W Credit Card	$825	$3,300
$175	N Car Insurance	$525	$2,100
$120	W Cell Phone	$360	$1,440
$100	W Cable	$300	$1,200
$100	W Personal Loan	$300	$1,200
$60	N Electric	$180	$720
$55	N Gas	$165	$660
$30	N Water	$90	$360
$2,835		**$8,505**	**$34,020**

Chapter 3: Understanding Your Expenses versus Income, we identified our monthly expenses and what we had left for our disposable income after all of the bills were paid. A couple of items here, if you shop around, can be significantly reduced or even cut in half. Let's look at the cable bill. This bill may include your cable and internet. Do you know what comes explicitly with your package you are paying for with your cable or dish provider? How often do you use it? If you are watching the content you can get from other sources for less cost, what would you be missing? I do not care much for TV, only live sports and movies. I can get everything else on TV for a lower cost through a streaming service. Identify what you and your family watch and start your search on who else offers a similar service. This process may take time as you are not looking to sacrifice, you are looking to improve the cost. Keep the internet

as I am sure that you will need it for streaming your services if you find a comparable deal. If you reduce your current bill by just 20%, the reduction would be more money added to your disposable income. This bill will be different for everyone based on their current package. If you notice you or your family spend most of the day watching TV, enjoy the local park, try some fun board games or a new hobby. Once you have found the service that maximizes your income and provides quality, you can safely move it for your finance team to begin managing the new bill. Every time you add to your bill account, always ensure it is for the long term and the best price to maximize your disposable income. When you have a low-cost, quality service that you plan on using for pretty much your lifetime, upgrade the W to an N. Make sure to adjust your direct deposit to reflect the change.

Cell phones are a big one, and this one might take some time. It took me almost a year for the perfect deal to plop on my lap, but when it did, I signed up immediately and saved 50% on my monthly bill, and got a new phone for free out of it. Cell phone companies compete for customers pretty hard. Almost every year around Black Friday, you can find that you can sign up somewhere to receive a free phone and a low-cost bill for the next two years. Spoiler alert they don't just hand out phones for you to jump to another company within a year. They also don't hand out the newest models either, but it will more than likely still be a great phone that can meet most of your needs. Wherever you start your search, make sure you choose a company that you can stay with for two years based on the deal they can offer. Most are offering unlimited, and some do have hidden fees where others don't, so make sure you read the fine print, ask questions, and if it makes sense, lock in the deal! If you don't want to wait around for them to give you the phone, you can buy one outright at the store or online. Again, the purpose here is to maintain your disposable income. Why pay monthly for a phone when you can work with your finance team to set it aside for you? Having a second account just for your bills has a lot of advantages. You will notice some cell phone companies offer a discount when you sign up for autopay, increasing your savings. Already have a phone? There is no need to wait to see who offers the best option to switch over while keeping your phone. This option should be an easy one! Once you have found the service that maximizes your income and provides quality, you can safely move it for your finance team to begin managing. Every time you add to your bill account, always ensure it is for the long term and the best price to maximize your disposable income. When you have a low-cost, quality service that you plan on using for pretty much your lifetime, upgrade the W to an N. Make sure to adjust your direct deposit to reflect the change.

Now car insurance is a need, and they do reward loyalty. This expense is something to consider when shopping around. Don't be fooled by the bundle either, as it is not always cost-effective to bundle your insurance with one company. They may offer a discount, but that doesn't mean they will be showing you the best price. When I was shopping for my home owner's insurance, I naturally called my car insurance company, eager to bundle and receive the discount! Sadly, it was much more than what I was willing to pay for with the deal. I ultimately went with another company who then offered to bundle my car insurance with my home owner's insurance. Their price for my car insurance with the discount was horrible. It was almost twice what I was paying for car insurance at the time. I remember laughing both times and mentioning how funny I thought it was how they advertise how much you can save when you bundle, but in reality, I would have paid double with both companies either way. One was better for car insurance and the other for homeowners. I think you get the point here. It costs you nothing to make a 15-minute phone call and see who can offer you the same quality service at a lower cost. You would be surprised how much you can save here. Also work with you finance team to set aside the amount needed for each term instead of monthly payments. Once you have that amount set aside you can save on the overall amount due by switching off monthly payments to bi-yearly or yearly payments.

You may not be able to reduce your mortgage. Still, if you rent, you can have an opportunity here to find a similar place not far from where you are and reduce your rent by 20%, or if you are now ready to purchase a home, you can start with a duplex where you become the landlord, and your tenant can pay your mortgage. If you aren't in the mood to share your space, consider looking for a home. My current home is 15 minutes from where I used to rent, and my mortgage is half of what I was paying in rent, and my house is more extensive. I have an enormous backyard, a more oversized front porch, and my house has additional square footage. Buying your first home is a lengthy process, and it is important to learn early on what preparations can assist you based on what you want to spend. Remember your disposable income. Be careful not to flex your full approval based on your gross income. It's your net income you live by when making payments and using your disposable income.

You purchase many things in your life, and you would be surprised at how much you can save based on where and how you buy. I am a big fan of Converse sneakers. Not the solid color sneakers. The sneakers unique with fancy designs. They typically go for $100 or more at the store. I usually pay no more than $25 for each pair. I didn't have to sacrifice anything. Shop around! It doesn't have to take all day, so enjoy the experience and make the most of what you learn for your long-term spending habits.

Most people I know are shocked to find out how much I spend on my bills monthly and even more shocked on what I spend on my personal effects, such as clothes, items for my home, and the bulk of my possessions—asked often is how to afford my lifestyle, which is an easy answer. I have learned many lessons from being in debt and have learned how to make better decisions to maximize my disposable income. I give in to temptation every so often but recover quickly from giving in once I recognize where the decision may lead. It doesn't take forever to make good decisions, and you don't have to wait forever to make a decision either. You should always be open to a good deal, and once you have that mindset, you will find good deals come to you even when you aren't looking. Ensure you have a good relationship with a friend or loved one who can be honest with you and keep you on the path you want to be on by holding you accountable to your goals. They will always serve as good reminders of what you have gone through and where you want to be.

Remember to leverage your credit union! You can downsize and reduce your debt by refinancing at a lower interest rate. If you qualify for a personal loan that can pay off your credit cards, you will pay far less interest which will pay off the debt faster. Your minimum payment accomplishes more when the interest is low as more of your money goes to the principal. This method is one of the best actions you can take to combine with other strategies but be careful. If you do not cut up the credit cards, you can easily dig a deeper hole in debt. Shop around and find the best interest rate that can beat what your interest rates currently are at now. Starting at the credit union is an easy trip as it costs you nothing, and you have a higher probability of being approved. This action alone can reduce payments and the amount of time-based on the loan length the credit union can support. You will start to realize it is not about cutting back but making better decisions with your money in the long term. Never sacrifice quality. Ensure you aren't missing out on the same or better experience for a lower price.

7

HOW LONG UNTIL I'M DEBT FREE?

"I may not be there yet but I'm closer than I was yesterday."

— UNKNOWN

As you have seen through these strategies, you can typically operate on a 3-month timeline which will help you check in with your plan and ensure you are meeting your goal. More importantly, every three months, you should be checking your bill account to see what your finance team has set aside for you. That amount can help speed up the process, be used to treat yourself, or provide some added comfort knowing you have some money set to the side in the event it is needed.

This rotation can also help you take an opportunity to check in with yourself to see where your mental and emotional space is as well.

To truly get an idea of how long the journey will take with making no changes to your income or your spending habits, take what you have left to spend for managing your life and divide it by half.

In our example, $1020 – what we have left to make decisions in managing life and debt would now be $510. Trying to do the math with your minimum payments won't give you a solid timeline as you pay interest. Example: Your credit card has a $7400 balance. If you were to divide $7400 by $320, you would get around 24 which is 24 months or two years; however, your credit card charges interest daily on the balance you carry each month. It will take you longer than two years due to the interest charges. I mentioned earlier in Chapter 3: Understanding Your Expenses versus Income that minimum payments alone are not enough to speed up the process, which is why we identify a specific amount we can send to debt in addition to the minimum payment. Now, if you take the $7400 and divide that by $510, you get roughly 14, so it would take a little over a year to pay off the credit card with the highest balance owed and highest minimum monthly payment. To build a timeline on the entire process, take your total debt of $51,650 and divide by what you can commit to sending to your debt monthly, which in this example is $510. This calculation is roughly around 100,

100 months, or a little over eight years. That is a long time to be in debt. If you use some of the strategies listed, all you have to do is update the amount you commit to debt. This exercise is the purpose behind managing your debt timeline three months at a time. You can list your long-term timeline based on your willingness to commit. As that changes, you should update it every three months to understand how your decisions are impacting your timeline. Also, consider if you were able to refinance your debt at a lower interest rate. Without sending additional money, that alone can bring your timeline down to a maximum of 5 years simply because that is the term of your new consolidated loan. As you start each strategy and make accomplishments in using them, always remember to celebrate your success. Each celebration brings you closer to the finale!

Monthly	Bill	TOTAL
$350	W Car	$18,000
$320	W Credit Card	$7,400
$300	W Personal Loan	$17,000
$275	W Credit Card	$5,000
$120	W Cell Phone	$850
$100	W Cable	0
$100	W Personal Loan	$3,400
$1,565		**$51,650**

Remember when we picked up a part-time job? This action would change your timeline based on what you could commit. If you also added in renting some of your space out, this impacts your timeline. Understanding your timeline can be a massive motivator in making your decisions. Knowing you can get something done in a shorter amount of time helps make the immense sacrifice of your time and space. It can also help you accept where you are and the length of time it will take without paying additional money to your debt. Let's build out some examples below to understand how you will reach your goal and the timeline it took you to accomplish. The purpose of this exercise is to know the length of time to pay off your debt ultimately.

	Monthly		Monthly
Full time/OT	$2,000	**Full time/OT W/Rent**	$2,500
Part time/OT	$1,000	**Part time/OT W/Rent**	$1,500
No 2nd job/OT	$510	**No 2nd job/OT**	$510

Ok, so eight years is a long time, but it represents the reality of how long it takes. Let's see what the other scenario's offer. Each time you pay off in full one of your debt items or increase your income, update your timeline based on what you can commit. You should check your bill account every three months as the amount over what is needed to pay for your bills should assist with paying off your debt.

Our benchmark is: a little over 8 years paying an additional $510

With a part time job:

$1,000+$510 = $1,510, $51,650/$1,510 =

34 months or a little under 3 years

A part time job with renting your space:

$1,500+$510 = $2,010, $51,650/$2,010 =

25 months or a little over 2 years

With a 2nd full-time job:

$2,000+$510 = $2,510, $51,650/$2,510 =

20 months or a under 2 years

A 2nd full-time job with renting your space:

$2,500+$510 = $3,010, $51,650/$3,010 =

17 months or less than 2 years!

The overall timeline changes as you pay off in full one of your debt items. Use the minimum payment from that debt you paid added to the amount you can send monthly. You can then update your timeline. Whenever your income increases, you should be updating the amount you can send to your debt and update your timeline. The example we used in Chapter 4: Strategies Based on Mentality & Emotion, we rotated different options every three months based on what we were willing to do and what we were ready to sacrifice. We also updated our amount each time you had a debt paid in full to include that minimum payment into the total amount we would commit to paying off our debt. You don't have to increase your income to pay your debt off; however, keep in mind the more you pay your debt, the faster you are out.

Leveraging your timeline is how you can accept the outcome of your decision. If it takes almost eight years with nothing changing, at least you know how long it will take you to reach your goal of getting out of debt. However, once you get an idea of what extra hours at work can contribute, or renting out your space and even cutting back on a few items, your mental space, and emotional space will be motivated to shorten your timeline. An extra 20 hours of working a week, whether overtime or a part-time job, cuts your timeline by more than half. Although you have to spend time shopping around, consolidation can have the second most significant impact as you lock a low-interest rate. Write down where you are now with what you can commit to your debt each month and see your timeline. Are you comfortable with that length of time and simply doing nothing?

8

MY REWARD? FOCUS AND REGROUP

"Effort only fully releases its reward after a person refuses to quit."

— NAPOLEON HILL

Depending on which road you took, either the climb or the snowball after the first three months, you might start asking yourself if the reward of being debt-free is worth it. Listen, if this were easy, no one would be in debt, right? First things first, ask yourself why am I doing this? You want to be free to enjoy your disposable income. Save for your children to go to college. Enjoy vacations and travel regularly. Improve your credit score and purchase a home. You are tired of arguing about money. Invest in yourself and what you want to experience! There are many reasons you want to do this, so make sure you write them down.

Keep them handy when the going gets tough, so you can keep going. Did you find your cheerleader? Someone in your life believes in you even if you don't think they do. Be vulnerable, practice humility, and share your journey and your goal. That person or group of people will help you stay focused and support you when you need to regroup. My sister and my friend were there for me constantly. I remember a few times they both had to talk me off the ledge of giving up, and I am incredibly grateful for their supportive words. When someone sees your effort and says they are proud of you, it can fill your confidence tank up and give you the boost you need to keep going. Sometimes we don't have enough faith in ourselves to conquer what we set out to do. Take that time to share that challenge with your cheerleader and let them cheer you on. Have you pictured what life will be like debt-free? Knowing why you are doing something and visualizing your goals are two different exercises. Imagine yourself stress-free and doing the things you are not doing because of your debt. What's the first thing you want to do when you are debt-free?

Maybe you want to celebrate and throw a party for yourself. Believe it or not but debt-free parties are a thing. Do you want to take an extended vacation to revel in the fruits of your labor? Plan it, see it, and think about it. Your brain is powerful, and when you set your mind on something, your actions and decisions will support it. If you dove in headfirst and realize you aren't swimming as strong as you could, there is nothing wrong with going back to the shallow end of the pool. If that full-time job hit you a little too hard, then pull back to something part-time and find out what you need to be successful full-time. If it was something that you didn't prepare for, you could take months 1-3 working part-time and focusing on getting yourself to full-time month 3-6 preparing for it with those first three months. The overall strategy to pay off your debt adjusts as you are on the journey. Please take advantage of that strategy and make it work for you to continue to shorten the length of time it takes to pay off your debt. You will learn so much about yourself while on this journey. You will see the adjustments you make, how they impact your overall goal, and how it will improve your financial stability long term. You don't have to wait for the walls to start caving in for you to focus and regroup. Every three months, you should be re-evaluating where you are in your journey and what you plan to do for the next three months. By maintaining the three-month cycle, you should continuously check in with yourself and be honest about what your mental and emotional space can handle when making your decisions. Think of it as a quarterly check-up. You can always include your cheerleader in that conversation, as their support can go a long way.

When I did my last check-in, I was eager to continue for another three months even though I had accomplished my goal simply because I wanted to build up a cushion of savings. After discussing it with my cheerleader, we realized that I no longer needed to sacrifice my time working two full-time jobs. I had already accomplished my goal and had built a cushion. Sometimes it's not about someone encouraging you to move forward but bringing you back to the reason you started this whole journey. That conversation was the reality check I needed, and I was grateful for the honesty I received. When you see all you can accomplish, you can sometimes get greedy, and usually, greed is what got us here in the first place. Having the finance team by my side, my decision-making has changed when it comes to my purchases and how I spend my money on wants. Focus on your immediate goal, regroup on the whole journey and keep imagining your reward!

You have come so far already! Some questions below to ask yourself that will keep you focused.

- First things first ask yourself why am I doing this?
- Did you find your cheerleader?
- Have you pictured what life will be like debt free?
- What's the first thing you want to do when you are debt free?

9

YOU'RE OUT NOW STAY OUT!

"Money is a tool. Used properly it makes something beautiful; used wrong, it makes a mess!"

— BRADLEY VINSON

You did it! Now what? Live your dreams out and make new goals but don't go overboard with your spending. Make sure you are maintaining your percentages and keep your options open. Maybe you're a homebody and don't go out much, so you increase your percentage of income versus expenses by over 30%. Just make sure you don't make any decisions you truly can't afford. This book should be your guide when staying out. During your journey, you should review the questions you asked yourself when making big purchases or signing up for something that will charge you monthly. The world is your oyster now, and with your improved mentality, you can make different decisions. One way to help you stay out is thinking about how you can share the costs of what you want. Invest in something that gives you money and increases your income. Passive income is one of the best investments you can make, as it generally does not require much of your time. You can invest in real estate, the stock market, and many things to increase your income without having to put in extra hours. There is good debt where you borrow money, and someone pays back the loan like in real estate. A loan on a rental property doesn't have to be paid by you but by your tenant. I encourage you to explore what's out there and make the most of investing in yourself. You shouldn't be surprised after reading this book what a good book can teach you, and it's a small investment upfront. As you embark on your new journey of being debt-free, remember to check in with yourself and your finance team every three months. The strategies here don't change when you are out of debt, as they will keep you out. You will experience temptation, and you will give in on some of these temptations. It's ok if this happens but, learn from it and prepare.

When I give in, it doesn't spiral out of control, and I don't dig a debt hole. Unexpected challenges will happen. Don't get caught burning through your credit card for a challenge that is simply an inconvenience. Overcome it when your budget works best in your favor. Rushing to overcome a challenge can quickly get you back into debt. A few weeks of working through the inconvenience can ensure you maintain a debt-free life. I have had quite a few unexpected challenges while I was on my journey. Still, I practiced humility and built stronger bonds and relationships with those around me, being vulnerable and asking for help. Everything is temporary until you can make it permanently work to your benefit.

Someone totaled my car while on my way to work. At the time, I didn't have 100% of what I usually spend on a vehicle. Instead of jumping into a loan, I asked a co-worker to carpool so I could focus on saving the money for another car. It took about two months, and, in the meantime, I had close family and friends bring me along for when they did their grocery shopping. The best part was everyone in my circle was all too happy to support me. I also spread the support so that I wouldn't put too much on one person. One co-worker carpooled, my family took turns bringing me with for the groceries, and another co-worker took me car shopping when I was ready. Having a cheerleader during your debt journey is different than working through a challenge. When getting hit with an inconvenience, people get it and are happier to help, knowing that you could quickly return the favor if it were to ever happen to them. This exercise of humility, learning, and preparation is how you stay out.

Reminders:

- Keep your percentage of income versus expenses at or around 30%
- Continue to check in with yourself and your finance team every 3 months
- Invest in yourself whether it be knowledge or passive income
- Don't rush to get into debt over an inconvenience
- Practice humility, be vulnerable and share with other so you can do the same for them in the future

I would be incredibly thankful if you could take 60 seconds to leave a brief review about your journey on Amazon. Sharing how this has helped you can help others in your situation even if it's a few sentences. I am excited to read about your results. Sharing is caring!

You can also join our Facebook Community - Bottoms Up Finance.

I created this group for everyone who is starting from the bottom of the debt hole to provide support from an entire community. Looking forward to meeting you!

CONCLUSION

You now have all the tools you need to get out of any debt situation. All of the examples provided work regardless of how deep in debt you are. You can easily calculate your timeline and your exit strategy to getting out of debt. It is easy to get into debt, but you can make it easy to stay out once you take the journey. Some of you will undoubtedly have more demanding journeys than others. No matter how arduous the journey is, know that you can accomplish anything you set your mind to achieve. Using the math provided in this book will help you with your decisions and give you a realistic view of how long it will take and what you need to do to take it. Always ask yourself the questions listed in this book and be honest with yourself. Many questions in each chapter are essential to think about as you start and end your journey in this book. Your financial stability is vital, so always think about your responses. You have everything to gain and nothing to lose by following these steps and making decisions that work best for you mentally and emotionally. I cannot express how empowering it is to live life not worrying about bills. That process all by itself, even if you choose not to take the debt journey, changes how you live your life and make decisions. You know the choices you made that brought you to this book, so remember those moments and continue to learn about you. Use the text, refer to it as often as you need, and take over the world and build your life debt-free! Remember, there is good debt and bad debt. I encourage you to learn about good debt to help you over time and increase your income.

All the questions asked in this book are listed below for your ultimate point of reference:

- Can I completely pay this balance off by my due date?
- Can I completely pay the balance off within 2 months paying half by my due date?
- How many feet do you have?
- What is the goal you hope to achieve?
- Ever heard of the phrase "disposable income"?
- What do you consider to be monthly expenses?
- How do you decide what you need versus what you want when thinking about your expenses?
- Have you been able to admit to yourself how you feel about your current reality?

- What are you willing to do to get out of debt?
- How quickly do you want your reality to change?
- Do you need to increase your income to achieve your goals?
- How much do you take home monthly? Quarterly? Yearly?
- How much do you spend on take out?
- Do you enjoy your own cooking?
- Do you find yourself throwing out food whether it expired or was old leftovers?
- What is about pre made meals or take out you enjoy most?
- Why is someone else's name more important than your goals?
- Who is paying your debt?
- How can you make your house work for you?
- What percentage should my monthly expenses be?
- How much disposable income do you want to enjoy?
- Ask yourself what do you need from your vehicle?
- If you tried to sell your car for what it is worth would it be enough to pay off the loan?
- Ask yourself what do you need your phone to do?
- Are you comfortable with that length of time simply by doing nothing?
- First things first ask yourself why am I doing this?
- Did you find your cheerleader?
- Have you pictured what life will be like debt free?

- What's the first thing you want to do when you are debt free?